501
CHALLENGING
LOGIC AND
REASONING
PROBLEMS

501 CHALLENGING LOGIC AND REASONING PROBLEMS

2nd Edition

LearningExpress®

NEW YORK

Library of Congress Cataloging-in-Publication Data:
   501 challenging logic & reasoning problems.
      p. cm.—(LearningExpress skill builders practice)
   Includes bibliographical references.
   ISBN 1-57685-534-1
   1. Logic—Problems, exercises, etc. 2. Reasoning—Problems, exercises, etc.
3. Critical thinking—Problems, exercises, etc. I. LearningExpress (Organization)
II. Title: 501 challenging logic and reasoning problems. III. Series.
BC108.A15 2006
160'.76—dc22

                                 2005057953

Printed in the United States of America

9 8 7 6 5 4 3 2

Second Edition

ISBN 10: 1-57685-534-1
ISBN 13: 978-1-57685-534-8

For information or to place an order, contact LearningExpress at:
   2 Rector Street
   26th Floor
   New York, NY 10006

Or visit us at:
   www.learnatest.com

Contents ▶

Introduction

This book—which can be used alone, with other logic and reasoning texts of your choice, or in combination with LearningExpress's *Reasoning Skills Success in 20 Minutes a Day*—will give you practice dealing with the types of multiple-choice questions that appear on standardized tests assessing logic, reasoning, judgment, and critical thinking. It is designed to be used by individuals working on their own and by teachers or tutors helping students learn, review, or practice basic logic and reasoning skills. Practice on 501 logic and reasoning questions will go a long way in alleviating test anxiety, too!

Maybe you're one of the millions of people who, as students in elementary or high school, never understood the necessity of having to read opinion essays and draw conclusions from the writer's argument. Or maybe you never understood why you had to work through all those verbal analogies or number series questions. Maybe you were one of those people who could never see a "plan of attack" when working through logic games or critical thinking puzzles. Or perhaps you could never see a connection between everyday life and analyzing evidence from a series of tedious reading passages. If you fit into one of these groups, this book is for you.

First, know you are not alone. It is true that some people relate more easily than do others to number series questions, verbal analogies, logic games, and reading passages that present an argument. And that's okay; we all have unique talents. Still, it's a fact that for most jobs today, critical thinking skills—including analytical and logical reasoning—are essential. The good news is that these skills can be developed with practice.

Learn by doing. It's an old lesson, tried and true. And it's the tool this book is designed to give you. The 501 logic and reasoning questions that follow will provide you with lots of practice. As you work through each set of questions, you'll be gaining a solid understanding of basic analytical and logical reasoning skills—all without memorizing! The purpose of this book is to help you improve your critical thinking through encouragement, no frustration.

▶ An Overview

501 Challenging Logic and Reasoning Problems is divided into 37 sets of questions:

Sets 1–4: Number Series
Sets 5–6: Letter and Symbol Series
Sets 7–8: Verbal Classification
Sets 9–11: Essential Part
Sets 12–17: Analogies
Sets 18–19: Artificial Language
Set 20: Matching Definitions
Set 21: Making Judgments
Set 22: Verbal Reasoning
Sets 23–27: Logic Problems
Sets 28–31: Logic Games
Sets 32–37: Analyzing Arguments

Each set contains between 5–20 questions, depending on their length and difficulty. The book is specifically organized to help you build confidence as you further develop your logic and reasoning skills. *501 Challenging Logic and Reasoning Problems* begins with basic number and letter series questions, and then moves on to verbal classification, artificial language, and matching definition items. The last sets contain logic problems, logic games, and logical reasoning questions. By the time you reach the last question, you'll feel confident that you've improved your critical thinking and logical reasoning abilities.

▶ How to Use This Book

Whether you're working alone or helping someone brush up his or her critical thinking and reasoning skills, this book will give you the opportunity to practice, practice, practice!

Working on Your Own

If you are working alone to improve your logic skills or prepare for a test in connection with a job or school, you will probably want to use this book in combination with its companion text, *Reasoning Skills Success in 20 Minutes a Day, 2nd Edition,* or with some other basic reasoning skills text. If you're fairly sure of your basic logic and reasoning abilities, however, you can use *501 Challenging Logic and Reasoning Problems* by itself.

Use the answer key at the end of the book not only to find out if you got the right answer, but also to learn how to tackle similar kinds of questions next time. Every answer is explained. Make sure you understand the explanations—usually by going back to the questions—before moving on to the next set.

Tutoring Others

This book will work well in combination with almost any analytical reasoning or logic text. You will probably find it most helpful to give students a brief lesson in the particular operation they'll be learning—number series, verbal classification, artificial language, logic problems, analyzing arguments—and then have them spend the remainder of the session actually answering the questions in the sets. You will want to stress the importance of learning by doing and of checking their answers and reading the explanations carefully. Make sure they understand a particular set of questions before you assign the next one.

▶ Additional Resources

Answering the 501 logic and reasoning questions in this book will give you lots of practice. Another way to improve your reasoning ability is to read and study on your own and devise your own unique methods of attacking logic problems. Following is a list of logic and reasoning books you may want to buy or take out of the library:

REASONING

Reasoning Skills Success in 20 Minutes a Day (2nd Edition) by LearningExpress

Critical Reasoning: A Practical Introduction by Anne Thomson (Routledge)

Attacking Faulty Reasoning: A Practical Guide to Fallacy-Free Arguments by T. Edward Damer (Wadsworth)

Thinking Critically: Techniques for Logical Reasoning by James H. Kiersky and Nicholas J. Caste (Wadsworth)

LOGIC

Essential Logic: Basic Reasoning Skills for the Twenty-First Century by Ronald C. Pine (Oxford University Press)

Increase Your Puzzle IQ: Tips and Tricks for Building Your Logic Power by Marcel Danesi (Wiley)

Amazing Logic Puzzles by Norman D. Willis (Sterling)

Challenging Logic Puzzles by Barry R. Clarke (Sterling)

CRITICAL THINKING

Critical Thinking by Alec Fisher (Cambridge University Press)

Brainplay: Challenging Puzzles & Thinking Games by Tom Werneck (Sterling)

Challenging Critical Thinking Puzzles by Michael A. Dispezio and Myron Miller (Sterling)

Becoming a Critical Thinker: A User-Friendly Manual by Sherry Diestler (Prentice Hall)

ANALOGIES

501 Word Analogy Questions by Learning-Express

Analogies for Beginners by Lynne Chatham (Dandy Lion Publications)

Cracking the MAT (3rd Edition) by Marcia Lerner (Princeton Review)

Questions ▶

Ready to test your mental abilities? Your 501 challenging logic and reasoning problems begin on the next page. They're grouped together in sets of 5–20 questions with a common theme. You can work through the sets in order or jump around, whichever you choose. When you finish a set, check your answers beginning on page 99.

▶ **Set 1** (Answers begin on page 99.)

Start off with these simple series of numbers. Number series questions measure your ability to reason without words. To answer these questions, you must determine the pattern of the numbers in each series before you will be able to choose which number comes next. These questions involve only simple arithmetic. Although most number series items progress by adding or subtracting, some questions involve simple multiplication or division. In each series, look for the degree and direction of change between the numbers. In other words, do the numbers increase or decrease, and by how much?

1. Look at this series: 2, 4, 6, 8, 10, . . . What number should come next?
a. 11
b. 12
c. 13
d. 14

2. Look at this series: 58, 52, 46, 40, 34, . . . What number should come next?
a. 26
b. 28
c. 30
d. 32

3. Look at this series: 40, 40, 47, 47, 54, . . . What number should come next?
a. 40
b. 44
c. 54
d. 61

4. Look at this series: 544, 509, 474, 439, . . . What number should come next?
a. 404
b. 414
c. 420
d. 445

5. Look at this series: 201, 202, 204, 207, . . . What number should come next?
a. 205
b. 208
c. 210
d. 211

6. Look at this series: 8, 22, 8, 28, 8, . . . What number should come next?
a. 9
b. 29
c. 32
d. 34

7. Look at this series: 80, 10, 70, 15, 60, . . . What number should come next?
a. 20
b. 25
c. 30
d. 50

8. Look at this series: 36, 34, 30, 28, 24, . . . What number should come next?
a. 20
b. 22
c. 23
d. 26

9. Look at this series: 22, 21, 23, 22, 24, 23, . . . What number should come next?
a. 22
b. 24
c. 25
d. 26

10. Look at this series: 3, 4, 7, 8, 11, 12, . . . What number should come next?
   a. 7
   b. 10
   c. 14
   d. 15

11. Look at this series: 31, 29, 24, 22, 17, . . . What number should come next?
   a. 15
   b. 14
   c. 13
   d. 12

12. Look at this series: 21, 9, 21, 11, 21, 13, . . . What number should come next?
   a. 14
   b. 15
   c. 21
   d. 23

13. Look at this series: 53, 53, 40, 40, 27, 27, . . . What number should come next?
   a. 12
   b. 14
   c. 27
   d. 53

14. Look at this series: 2, 6, 18, 54, . . . What number should come next?
   a. 108
   b. 148
   c. 162
   d. 216

15. Look at this series: 1,000, 200, 40, . . . What number should come next?
   a. 8
   b. 10
   c. 15
   d. 20

16. Look at this series: 7, 10, 8, 11, 9, 12, . . . What number should come next?
   a. 7
   b. 10
   c. 12
   d. 13

17. Look at this series: 14, 28, 20, 40, 32, 64, . . . What number should come next?
   a. 52
   b. 56
   c. 96
   d. 128

18. Look at this series: 1.5, 2.3, 3.1, 3.9, . . . What number should come next?
   a. 4.2
   b. 4.4
   c. 4.7
   d. 5.1

19. Look at this series: 5.2, 4.8, 4.4, 4, . . . What number should come next?
   a. 3
   b. 3.3
   c. 3.5
   d. 3.6

20. Look at this series: 2, 1, $\frac{1}{2}$, $\frac{1}{4}$, . . . What number should come next?
   a. $\frac{1}{3}$
   b. $\frac{1}{8}$
   c. $\frac{2}{8}$
   d. $\frac{1}{16}$

▶ Set 2 (Answers begin on page 101.)

This set contains additional, and sometimes more difficult, number series questions. Again, each question has a definite pattern. Some of the number series may be interrupted by a particular number that appears periodically in the pattern. For example, in the series 14, 16, 32, 18, 20, 32, 22, 24, 32, the number 32 appears as every third number. Sometimes, the pattern contains two alternating series. For example, in the series 1, 5, 3, 7, 5, 9, 7, the pattern is add 4, subtract 2, add 4, subtract 2, and so on. Look carefully for the pattern, and then choose which *pair* of numbers comes next. Note also that you will be choosing from five options instead of four.

21. 84 78 72 66 60 54 48
   a. 44 34
   b. 42 36
   c. 42 32
   d. 40 34
   e. 38 32

22. 3 8 13 18 23 28 33
   a. 39 44
   b. 38 44
   c. 38 43
   d. 37 42
   e. 33 38

23. 20 20 17 17 14 14 11
   a. 8 8
   b. 11 11
   c. 11 14
   d. 8 9
   e. 11 8

24. 18 21 25 18 29 33 18
   a. 43 18
   b. 41 44
   c. 37 18
   d. 37 41
   e. 38 41

25. 9 11 33 13 15 33 17
   a. 19 33
   b. 33 35
   c. 33 19
   d. 15 33
   e. 19 21

26. 2 8 14 20 26 32 38
   a. 2 46
   b. 44 50
   c. 42 48
   d. 40 42
   e. 32 26

27. 28 25 5 21 18 5 14
   a. 11 5
   b. 10 7
   c. 11 8
   d. 5 10
   e. 10 5

28. 9 12 11 14 13 16 15
   a. 14 13
   b. 18 21
   c. 14 17
   d. 12 13
   e. 18 17

29. 75 65 85 55 45 85 35
   a. 25 15
   b. 25 85
   c. 35 25
   d. 85 35
   e. 25 75

30. 1 10 7 20 13 30 19
  a. 26 40
  b. 29 36
  c. 40 25
  d. 25 31
  e. 40 50

31. 10 20 25 35 40 50 55
  a. 70 65
  b. 60 70
  c. 60 75
  d. 60 65
  e. 65 70

32. 40 40 31 31 22 22 13
  a. 13 4
  b. 13 5
  c. 4 13
  d. 9 4
  e. 4 4

33. 17 17 34 20 20 31 23
  a. 26 23
  b. 34 20
  c. 23 33
  d. 27 28
  e. 23 28

34. 2 3 4 5 6 4 8
  a. 9 10
  b. 4 8
  c. 10 4
  d. 9 4
  e. 8 9

35. 61 57 50 61 43 36 61
  a. 29 61
  b. 27 20
  c. 31 61
  d. 22 15
  e. 29 22

36. 9 16 23 30 37 44 51
  a. 59 66
  b. 56 62
  c. 58 66
  d. 58 65
  e. 54 61

37. 8 22 12 16 22 20 24
  a. 28 32
  b. 28 22
  c. 22 28
  d. 32 36
  e. 22 26

38. 6 20 8 14 10 8 12
  a. 14 10
  b. 2 18
  c. 4 12
  d. 2 14
  e. 14 14

39. 11 16 21 26 31 36 41
  a. 47 52
  b. 46 52
  c. 45 49
  d. 46 51
  e. 46 52

40. 8 11 21 15 18 21 22
  a. 25 18
  b. 25 21
  c. 25 29
  d. 24 21
  e. 22 26

▶ **Set 3** (Answers begin on page 102.)

This set will give you additional practice dealing with number series questions.

41. 44 41 38 35 32 29 26
 a. 24 21
 b. 22 19
 c. 23 19
 d. 29 32
 e. 23 20

42. 6 10 14 18 22 26 30
 a. 36 40
 b. 33 37
 c. 38 42
 d. 34 36
 e. 34 38

43. 34 30 26 22 18 14 10
 a. 8 6
 b. 6 4
 c. 14 18
 d. 6 2
 e. 4 0

44. 2 44 4 41 6 38 8
 a. 10 12
 b. 35 32
 c. 34 9
 d. 35 10
 e. 10 52

45. 32 29 26 23 20 17 14
 a. 11 8
 b. 12 8
 c. 11 7
 d. 32 29
 e. 10 9

46. 14 14 26 26 38 38 50
 a. 60 72
 b. 50 62
 c. 50 72
 d. 62 62
 e. 62 80

47. 8 12 9 13 10 14 11
 a. 14 11
 b. 15 12
 c. 8 15
 d. 15 19
 e. 8 5

48. 4 7 26 10 13 20 16
 a. 14 4
 b. 14 17
 c. 18 14
 d. 19 13
 e. 19 14

49. 3 8 10 15 17 22 24
 a. 26 28
 b. 29 34
 c. 29 31
 d. 26 31
 e. 26 32

50. 17 14 14 11 11 8 8
 a. 8 5
 b. 5 2
 c. 8 2
 d. 5 5
 e. 5 8

51. 13 29 15 26 17 23 19
 a. 21 23
 b. 20 21
 c. 20 17
 d. 25 27
 e. 22 20

52. 16 26 56 36 46 68 56
  a. 80 66
  b. 64 82
  (c.) 66 80
  d. 78 68
  e. 66 82

53. 7 9 66 12 14 66 17
  (a.) 19 66
  b. 66 19
  c. 19 22
  d. 20 66
  e. 66 20

54. 3 5 35 10 12 35 17
  a. 22 35
  b. 35 19
  (c.) 19 35
  d. 19 24
  e. 22 24

55. 36 31 29 24 22 17 15
  a. 13 11
  b. 10 5
  c. 13 8
  d. 12 7
  (e.) 10 8

56. 42 40 38 35 33 31 28 26 24
  a. 25 22
  b. 26 23
  (c.) 26 24
  d. 25 23
  e. 26 22

57. 11 14 14 17 17 20 20
  (a.) 23 23
  b. 23 26
  c. 21 24
  d. 24 24
  e. 24 27

58. 17 32 19 29 21 26 23 25
  a. 25 25
  b. 20 22
  (c.) 23 25
  d. 25 22
  e. 27 32

59. 10 34 12 31 14 28 16 25 18
  (a.) 25 18
  b. 30 13
  c. 19 26
  d. 18 20
  e. 25 22

60. 32 31 32 29 32 27 32
  (a.) 25 32
  b. 31 32
  c. 29 32
  d. 25 30
  e. 29 30

Perfect!

▶ **Set 4** (Answers begin on page 103.)

This set contains additional number series questions, some of which are in Roman numerals. These items differ from Sets 1, 2, and 3 because they ask you to find the number that fits somewhere into the *middle* of the series. Some of the items involve both numbers and letters; for these questions, look for a number series *and* a letter series. (For additional practice in working letter series questions, see Set 5.)

61. Look at this series: 8, 43, 11, 41, __, 39, 17, . . .
What number should fill in the blank?
   a. 8
   b. 14
   c. 43
   d. 44

62. Look at this series: 15, __, 27, 27, 39, 39, . . .
What number should fill the blank?
   a. 51
   b. 39
   c. 23
   d. 15

63. Look at this series: 83, 73, 93, 63, __, 93, 43, . . .
What number should fill the blank?
   a. 33
   b. 53
   c. 73
   d. 93

64. Look at this series: 4, 7, 25, 10, __, 20, 16, 19, . . .
What number should fill the blank?
   a. 13
   b. 15
   c. 20
   d. 28

65. Look at this series: 72, 76, 73, 77, 74, __, 75, . . .
What number should fill the blank?
   a. 70
   b. 71
   c. 75
   d. 78

66. Look at this series: 70, 71, 76, __, 81, 86, 70, 91, . . .
What number should fill the blank?
   a. 70
   b. 71
   c. 80
   d. 96

67. Look at this series: 664, 332, 340, 170, __, 89, . . .
What number should fill the blank?
   a. 85
   b. 97
   c. 109
   d. 178

68. Look at this series: 0.15, 0.3, __, 1.2, 2.4, . . .
What number should fill the blank?
   a. 4.8
   b. 0.006
   c. 0.6
   d. 0.9

69. Look at this series: $\frac{1}{9}$, $\frac{1}{3}$, 1, __, 9, . . . What number should fill the blank?
   a. $\frac{2}{3}$
   b. 3
   c. 6
   d. 27

70. Look at this series: U32, V29, __, X23, Y20, . . .
What number should fill the blank?
   a. W26
   b. W17
   c. Z17
   d. Z26

71. Look at this series: J14, L16, __, P20, R22, . . .
What number should fill the blank?
a. S24
b. N18
c. M18
d. T24

72. Look at this series: F2, __, D8, C16, B32, . . .
What number should fill the blank?
a. A16
b. G4
c. E4
d. E3

73. Look at this series: V, VIII, XI, XIV, __, XX, . . .
What number should fill the blank?
a. IX
b. XXIII
c. XV
d. XVII

74. Look at this series: XXIV, XX, __, XII, VIII, . . .
What number should fill the blank?
a. XXII
b. XIII
c. XVI
d. IV

75. Look at this series: VI, 10, V, 11, __, 12, III, . . .
What number should fill the blank?
a. II
b. IV
c. IX
d. 14

Perfect!

► Set 5 (Answers begin on page 104.)

Another type of sequence question involves a series of letters in a pattern. Usually, these questions use the letters' alphabetical order as a base. To make matters more complicated, sometimes subscript numbers will be thrown into the letter sequence. In these series, you will be looking at both the letter pattern and the number pattern. Some of these questions ask you to fill the blank in the middle of the series; others ask you to add to the end of the series.

76. QPO NML KJI _____ EDC
a. HGF
b. CAB
c. JKL
d. GHI

77. JAK KBL LCM MDN _____
a. OEP
b. NEO
c. MEN
d. PFQ

78. B_2CD _____ BCD_4 B_5CD BC_6D
a. B_2C_2D
b. BC_3D
c. B_2C_3D
d. BCD_7

79. ELFA GLHA ILJA _____ MLNA
a. OLPA
b. KLMA
c. LLMA
d. KLLA

80. P_5QR P_4QS P_3QT _____ PQV
a. PQW
b. PQV_2
c. P_2QU
d. PQ_3U

81. CMM EOO GQQ _____ KUU
a. GRR
b. GSS
c. ISS
d. ITT

82. QAR RAS SAT TAU _____
a. UAV
b. UAT
c. TAS
d. TAT

83. DEF DEF_2 DE_2F_2 _____ $D_2E_2F_3$
a. DEF_3
b. D_3EF_3
c. D_2E_3F
d. $D_2E_2F_2$

84. SCD TEF UGH _____ WKL
a. CMN
b. UJI
c. VIJ
d. IJT

85. FAG GAF HAI IAH _____
a. JAK
b. HAL
c. HAK
d. JAI

86. BCB DED FGF HIH _____
a. JKJ
b. HJH
c. IJI
d. JHJ

87. ZA_5 Y_4B XC_6 W_3D _____
a. E_7V
b. V_2E
c. VE_5
d. VE_7

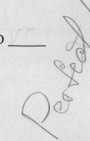

▶ Set 6 (Answers begin on page 105.)

This set contains sequence questions that use a series of nonverbal, nonnumber symbols. Look carefully at the sequence of symbols to find the pattern.

88.

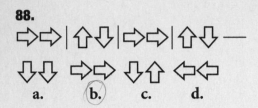

a.　b.　c.　d.

89.

a.　b.　c.　d.

90.

a.　b.　c.　d.

91.

a.　b.　c.　d.

92.

a.　b.　c.　d.

93.

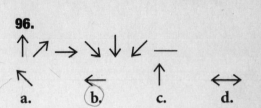

a.　b.　c.　d.

94.

a.　b.　c.　d.

95.

a.　b.　c.　d.

96.

a.　b.　c.　d.

97.

BBBB | BBBB | BBBB | BB —

BB　BB　BB　BB
a.　b.　c.　d.

98.

a.　b.　c.　d.

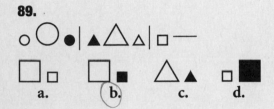

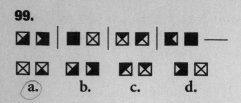

99.

a. b. c. d.

101.

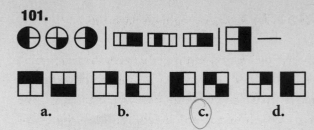

a. b. c. d.

100.

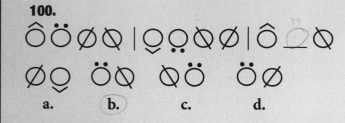

a. b. c. d.

▶ Set 7 (Answers begin on page 106.)

The next two sets contain verbal classification questions. For these questions, the important thing (as the name "verbal classification" indicates) is to *classify* the words in the four answer choices. Three of the words will be in the same classification; the remaining one will not be. Your answer will be the one word that does NOT belong in the same classification as the others.

102. Which word does NOT belong with the others?
a. leopard
b. cougar
c. elephant
d. lion

103. Which word does NOT belong with the others?
a. couch
b. rug
c. table
d. chair

104. Which word does NOT belong with the others?
a. tape
b. twine
c. cord
d. yarn

105. Which word does NOT belong with the others?
a. guitar
b. flute
c. violin
d. cello

106. Which word does NOT belong with the others?
a. tulip
b. rose
c. bud
d. daisy

107. Which word does NOT belong with the others?
a. tire
b. steering wheel
c. engine
d. car

108. Which word does NOT belong with the others?
a. parsley
b. basil
c. dill
d. mayonnaise

109. Which word does NOT belong with the others?
a. branch
b. dirt
c. leaf
d. root

110. Which word does NOT belong with the others?
a. unimportant
b. trivial
c. insignificant
d. familiar

111. Which word does NOT belong with the others?
a. book
b. index
c. glossary
d. chapter

112. Which word does NOT belong with the others?
a. noun
b. preposition
c. punctuation
d. adverb

113. Which word does NOT belong with the others?
a. cornea
b. retina
c. pupil
d. vision

114. Which word does NOT belong with the others?
a. rye
b. sourdough
c. pumpernickel
d. loaf

115. Which word does NOT belong with the others?
a. inch
b. ounce
c. centimeter
d. yard

116. Which word does NOT belong with the others?
a. street
b. freeway
c. interstate
d. expressway

117. Which word does NOT belong with the others?
a. dodge
b. flee
c. duck
d. avoid

118. Which word does NOT belong with the others?
a. heading
b. body
c. letter
d. closing

▶ **Set 8** (Answers begin on page 123.)

Here's another set of classification questions. Remember, you are looking for the word that does NOT belong in the same group as the others. Sometimes, all four words seem to fit in the same group. If so, look more closely to further narrow your classification.

119. Which word does NOT belong with the others?
a. core
b. seeds
c. pulp
d. slice

120. Which word does NOT belong with the others?
a. unique
b. beautiful
c. rare
d. exceptional

121. Which word does NOT belong with the others?
a. biology
b. chemistry
c. theology
d. zoology

122. Which word does NOT belong with the others?
a. triangle
b. circle
c. oval
d. sphere

123. Which word does NOT belong with the others?
a. excite
b. flourish
c. prosper
d. thrive

124. Which word does NOT belong with the others?
a. evaluate
b. assess
c. appraise
d. instruct

125. Which word does NOT belong with the others?
a. eel
b. lobster
c. crab
d. shrimp

126. Which word does NOT belong with the others?
a. scythe
b. knife
c. pliers
d. saw

127. Which word does NOT belong with the others?
a. two
b. three
c. six
d. eight

128. Which word does NOT belong with the others?
a. peninsula
b. island
c. bay
d. cape

129. Which word does NOT belong with the others?
a. seat
b. rung
c. cushion
d. leg

130. Which word does NOT belong with the others?
  a. fair
  b. just
  c. equitable
  d. favorable

131. Which word does NOT belong with the others?
  a. defendant
  b. prosecutor
  c. trial
  d. judge

132. Which word does NOT belong with the others?
  a. area
  b. variable
  c. circumference
  d. quadrilateral

133. Which word does NOT belong with the others?
  a. mayor
  b. lawyer
  c. governor
  d. senator

134. Which word does NOT belong with the others?
  a. acute
  b. right
  c. obtuse
  d. parallel

135. Which word does NOT belong with the others?
  a. wing
  b. fin
  c. beak
  d. rudder

136. Which word does NOT belong with the others?
  a. aorta
  b. heart
  c. liver
  d. stomach

▶ **Set 9** (Answers begin on page 108.)

In the next three sets, you will be looking for the essential part of something. Each question has an underlined word followed by four answer choices. You will choose the word that is a *necessary* part of the underlined word. A good way to approach this type of question is to say the following sentence: "A _____ could not exist without _____." Put the underlined word in the first blank. Try each of the answer choices in the second blank to see which choice is most logical.

For questions 137 through 151, find the word that names a *necessary* part of the underlined word.

137. book
   a. fiction
   b. pages
   c. pictures
   d. learning

138. guitar
   a. band
   b. teacher
   c. songs
   d. strings

139. shoe
   a. sole
   b. leather
   c. laces
   d. walking

140. respiration
   a. mouth
   b. circulation
   c. oxygen
   d. carbon monoxide

141. election
   a. president
   b. voter
   c. November
   d. nation

142. diploma
   a. principal
   b. curriculum
   c. employment
   d. graduation

143. swimming
   a. pool
   b. bathing suit
   c. water
   d. life jacket

144. school
   a. student
   b. report card
   c. test
   d. learning

145. language
   a. tongue
   b. slang
   c. writing
   d. words

146. desert
   a. cactus
   b. arid
   c. oasis
   d. flat

147. lightning
   a. electricity
   b. thunder
   c. brightness
   d. rain

148. <u>monopoly</u>
- **a.** corrupt
- **b.** exclusive
- **c.** rich
- **d.** gigantic

149. <u>harvest</u>
- **a.** autumn
- **b.** stockpile
- **c.** tractor
- **d.** crop

150. <u>gala</u>
- **a.** celebration
- **b.** tuxedo
- **c.** appetizer
- **d.** orator

151. <u>pain</u>
- **a.** cut
- **b.** burn
- **c.** nuisance
- **d.** hurt

▶ **Set 10** (Answers begin on page 109.)

Remember, you are looking for the essential part of something. If you had trouble with Set 9, go back through the items and study each answer explanation. Then work through this set of more difficult necessary part questions.

For questions 152 through 166, find the word that names a *necessary* part of the underlined word.

152. infirmary
   a. surgery
   b. disease
   c. patient
   d. receptionist

153. facsimile
   a. picture
   b. image
   c. mimeograph
   d. copier

154. domicile
   a. tenant
   b. dwelling
   c. kitchen
   d. house

155. culture
   a. civility
   b. education
   c. agriculture
   d. customs

156. bonus
   a. reward
   b. raise
   c. cash
   d. employer

157. antique
   a. rarity
   b. artifact
   c. aged
   d. prehistoric

158. itinerary
   a. map
   b. route
   c. travel
   d. guidebook

159. orchestra
   a. violin
   b. stage
   c. musician
   d. soloist

160. knowledge
   a. school
   b. teacher
   c. textbook
   d. learning

161. dimension
   a. compass
   b. ruler
   c. inch
   d. measure

162. sustenance
   a. nourishment
   b. water
   c. grains
   d. menu

163. ovation
   a. outburst
   b. bravo
   c. applause
   d. encore

164. <u>vertebrate</u>
 a. backbone
 b. reptile
 c. mammal
 d. animal

165. <u>provisions</u>
 a. groceries
 b. supplies
 c. gear
 d. caterers

166. <u>purchase</u>
 a. trade
 b. money
 c. bank
 d. acquisition

▶ **Set 11** (Answers begin on page 111.)

Here is one more set of necessary part questions. This set is somewhat more difficult than the previous two sets, and it should give you practice in mastering this particular type of question. Remember: A good way to approach this type of question is to use the following sentence: "A _____ could not exist without _____."

For questions 167 through 181, find the word that names a *necessary* part of the underlined word.

167. dome
   a. rounded
   b. geodesic
   c. governmental
   d. coppery

168. recipe
   a. desserts
   b. directions
   c. cookbook
   d. utensils

169. hurricane
   a. beach
   b. cyclone
   c. damage
   d. wind

170. autograph
   a. athlete
   b. actor
   c. signature
   d. pen

171. town
   a. residents
   b. skyscrapers
   c. parks
   d. libraries

172. wedding
   a. love
   b. church
   c. ring
   d. marriage

173. faculty
   a. buildings
   b. textbooks
   c. teachers
   d. meetings

174. cage
   a. enclosure
   b. prisoner
   c. animal
   d. zoo

175. directory
   a. telephone
   b. listing
   c. computer
   d. names

176. contract
   a. agreement
   b. document
   c. written
   d. attorney

177. saddle
   a. horse
   b. seat
   c. stirrups
   d. horn

178. vibration
   a. motion
   b. electricity
   c. science
   d. sound

179. <u>cell</u>
    a. chlorophyll
    b. nucleus
    c. nerve
    d. human

180. <u>champion</u>
    a. running
    b. swimming
    c. winning
    d. speaking

181. <u>glacier</u>
    a. mountain
    b. winter
    c. prehistory
    d. ice

▶ **Set 12** (Answers begin on page 113.)

Here is the first of several sets of analogies. Analogies test your ability to see relationships between words, objects, or concepts. There are many different types of analogy relationships: use or function, part-to-whole, classification, proportion or degree, cause and effect, similarity or difference. In each of these verbal analogies, you will be given a set of two related words, followed by a third word and four answer choices. Of the four choices, you must identify the one that would best complete the second set so that it expresses the same relationship as the first set. A good way to figure out the relationship in a given question is to make up a sentence that describes the relationship between the first two words. Then, try to use the same sentence to find out which of the answer choices completes the same relationship with the third word.

182. Cup is to coffee as bowl is to
  a. dish.
  b. soup.
  c. spoon.
  d. food.

183. Exercise is to gym as eating is to
  a. food.
  b. dieting.
  c. fitness.
  d. restaurant.

184. Oar is to rowboat as foot is to
  a. running.
  b. sneaker.
  c. skateboard.
  d. jumping.

185. Window is to pane as book is to
  a. novel.
  b. glass.
  c. cover.
  d. page.

186. Secretly is to openly as silently is to
  a. scarcely.
  b. impolitely.
  c. noisily.
  d. quietly.

187. Artist is to painting as senator is to
  a. attorney.
  b. law.
  c. politician.
  d. constituents.

188. Play is to actor as concert is to
  a. symphony.
  b. musician.
  c. piano.
  d. percussion.

189. Careful is to cautious as boastful is to
  a. arrogant.
  b. humble.
  c. joyful.
  d. suspicious.

190. Pride is to lion as school is to
  a. teacher.
  b. student.
  c. self-respect.
  d. fish.

191. Guide is to direct as reduce is to
  a. decrease.
  b. maintain.
  c. increase.
  d. preserve.

192. Yard is to inch as quart is to
   a. gallon.
   b. ounce.
   c. milk.
   d. liquid.

193. Reptile is to lizard as flower is to
   a. petal.
   b. stem.
   c. daisy.
   d. alligator.

194. Elated is to despondent as enlightened is to
   a. aware.
   b. ignorant.
   c. miserable.
   d. tolerant.

195. Marathon is to race as hibernation is to
   a. winter.
   b. bear.
   c. dream.
   d. sleep.

196. Embarrassed is to humiliated as frightened is to
   a. terrified.
   b. agitated.
   c. courageous.
   d. reckless.

197. Odometer is to mileage as compass is to
   a. speed.
   b. hiking.
   c. needle.
   d. direction.

198. Optimist is to cheerful as pessimist is to
   a. gloomy.
   b. mean.
   c. petty.
   d. helpful.

199. Sponge is to porous as rubber is to
   a. massive.
   b. solid.
   c. elastic.
   d. inflexible.

200. Candid is to indirect as honest is to
   a. frank.
   b. wicked.
   c. truthful.
   d. untruthful.

201. Pen is to poet as needle is to
   a. thread.
   b. button.
   c. sewing.
   d. tailor.

▶ **Set 13** (Answers begin on page 115.)

Now that you have some practice working basic analogies, try these picture analogies, which will give you practice with nonverbal reasoning. Solve these picture analogies in the same way you solved the word analogies. For each item, you will be presented with a set of two pictures that are related to each other in the same way. Along with this pair, you'll be given a third picture and four answer choices, which are also pictures. Of the four choices, choose the picture that would go in the empty box so that the two bottom pictures are related in the same way as the top two are related.

203.

a.　　　　b.　　　　c.　　　　d.

202.

a.　　　　b.　　　　c.　　　　d.

204.

a.　　　　b.　　　　c.　　　　d.

205.

206.

207.

208.

209.

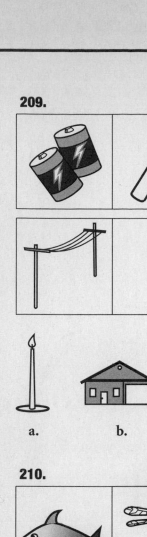

a.   b.   c.   d.

210.

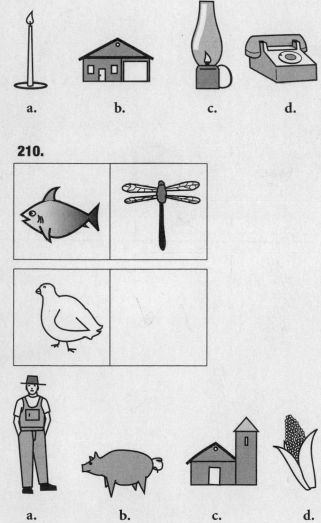

a.   b.   c.   d.

211.

a.   b.   c.   d.

212.

a.   b.   c.   d.

213.

a.   b.   c.   d.

215.

a.   b.   c.   d.

214.

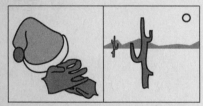

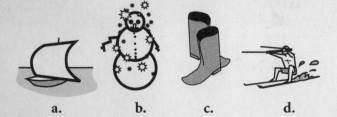

a.   b.   c.   d.

216.

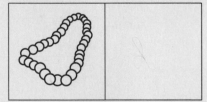

a.   b.   c.   d.

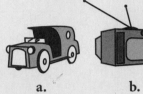

217.

a.   b.   c.   d.

218.

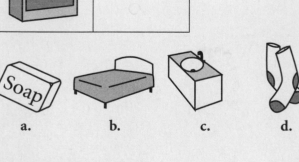

a.   b.   c.   d.

219.

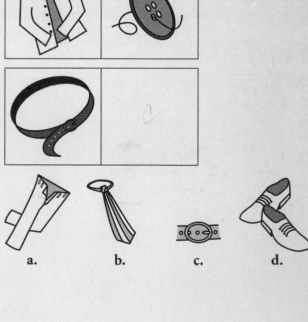

a.   b.   c.   d.

220.

a.   b.   c.   d.

221.

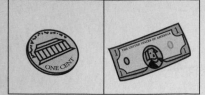

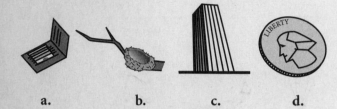

a.   b.   c.   d.

▶ **Set 14** (Answers begin on page 116.)

Here are more picture analogies for you to master. There is essentially no difference between verbal and picture analogies, except that you have to take an extra first step by naming each picture. Make sure you understand the relationship between the first set of pictures before you attempt to choose an answer. Make up a sentence that describes this relationship. From the four answer choices, choose the picture that would go in the empty box so that the two bottom pictures are related in the same way as the top two are related.

222.

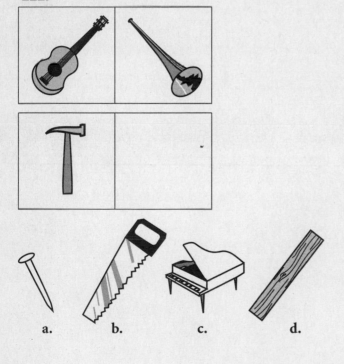

a.   b.   c.   d.

223.

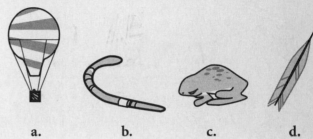

a.   b.   c.   d.

224.

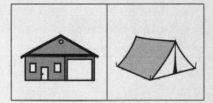

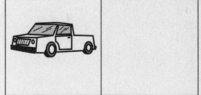

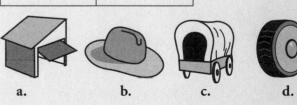

a.   b.   c.   d.

225.

a.   b.   c.   d.

226.

a.   b.   c.   d.

227.

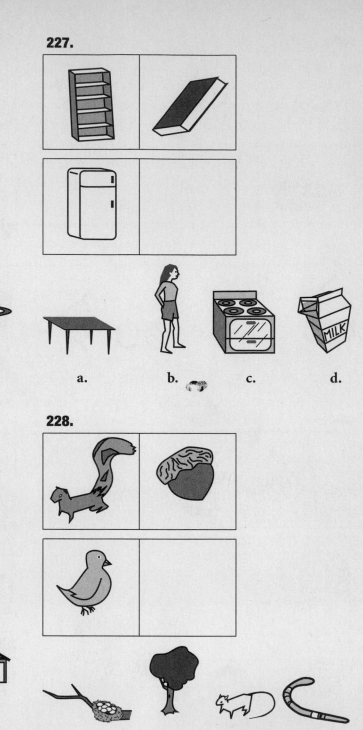

a.   b.   c.   d.

228.

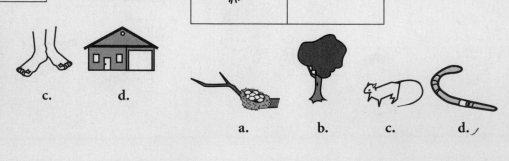

a.   b.   c.   d.

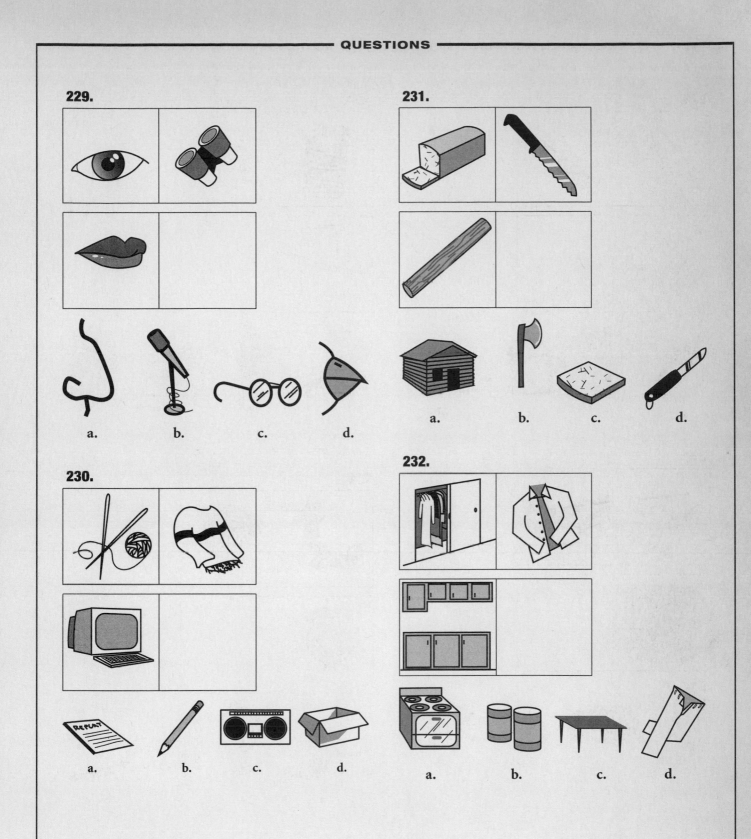

229.

a.   b.   c.   d.

230.

a.   b.   c.   d.

231.

a.   b.   c.   d.

232.

a.   b.   c.   d.

233.

235.

234.

236.

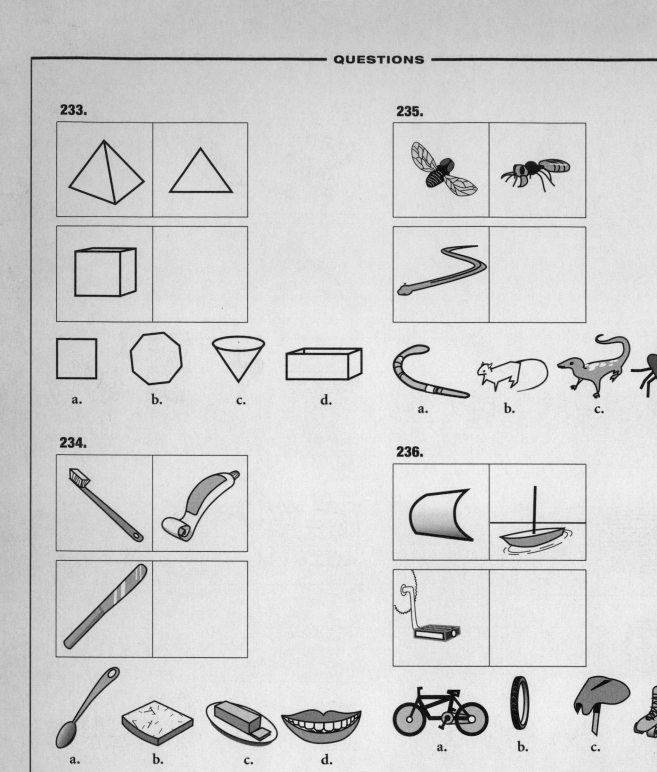

237.

a.   b.   c.   d.

239.

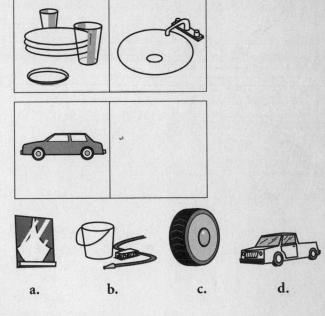

a.   b.   c.   d.

238.

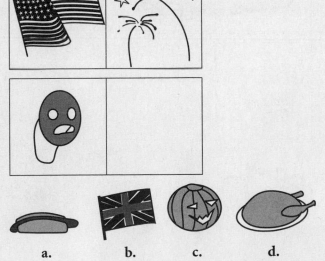

a.   b.   c.   d.

240.

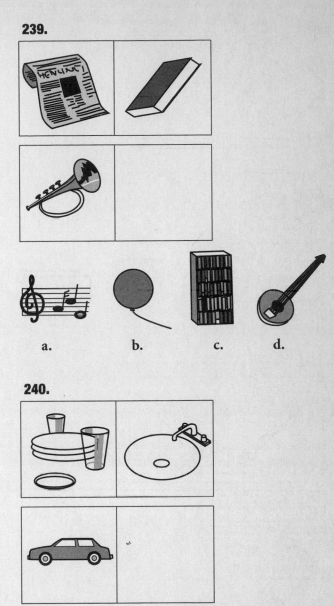

a.   b.   c.   d.

241.

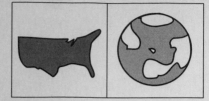

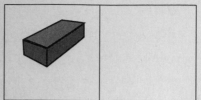

a.   b.   c.   d.

► **Set 15** (Answers begin on page 117.)

This set contains another type of verbal analogy questions. In each, the words in the top row are related in some way. To help you discover this relationship, make up a sentence based on the top three words. The words in the bottom row are related in the same way as the words in the top row. For each item, find the word that completes the bottom row of words.

242. ant   fly   bee

     hamster   squirrel   _____
- **a.** spider
- **b.** mouse
- **c.** rodent
- **d.** cat

243. carpenter   saw   nails

     pediatrician   stethoscope   _____
- **a.** thermometer
- **b.** baby
- **c.** doctor
- **d.** illness

244. table   wood   oak

     shirt   cloth   _____
- **a.** sewing
- **b.** dress
- **c.** cotton
- **d.** tree

245. rule   command   dictate

     doze   sleep   _____
- **a.** snore
- **b.** govern
- **c.** awaken
- **d.** hibernate

246. meal   banquet   feast

     shelter   palace   _____
- **a.** mansion
- **b.** hallway
- **c.** protection
- **d.** haven

247. fence   wall   boundary

     path   alley   _____
- **a.** ramp
- **b.** passageway
- **c.** airfield
- **d.** pedestrian

248. palette   easel   brush

     textbook   lesson plan   _____
- **a.** artist
- **b.** teacher
- **c.** report card
- **d.** paint

249. snow   mountain   ski

     warmth   lake   _____
- **a.** sand
- **b.** swim
- **c.** sunburn
- **d.** vacation

250. candle   lamp   floodlight

     hut   cottage   _____
- **a.** tent
- **b.** city
- **c.** dwelling
- **d.** house

251. apples   fruit   supermarket

novel   book   _____
a. bookstore
b. magazine
c. vegetable
d. shopping

252. tadpole   frog   amphibian

lamb   sheep   _____
a. animal
b. wool
c. farm
d. mammal

253. walk   skip   run

toss   pitch   _____
a. swerve
b. hurl
c. jump
d. dance

254. honeybee   angel   bat

kangaroo   rabbit   _____
a. mermaid
b. possum
c. grasshopper
d. sprinter

255. daisy   flower   plant

bungalow   house   _____
a. building
b. cottage
c. apartment
d. city

▶ **Set 16** (Answers begin on page 118.)

The next two sets will give you more practice with analogies. Every one of the following questions consists of a related pair of words, followed by five pairs of words labeled **a** through **e**. Choose the pair that *best* represents a similar relationship to the one expressed in the original pair of words. Remember, the best way to approach an analogy question is to make up a sentence that describes the relationship between the first two words. Then, find the pair that has a similar relationship.

256. PETAL : FLOWER
   a. salt : pepper
   b. tire : bicycle
   c. base : ball
   d. sandals : shoes
   e. puppy : dog

257. BRISTLE : BRUSH
   a. arm : leg
   b. stage : curtain
   c. recline : chair
   d. key : piano
   e. art : sculpture

258. FISH : SCHOOL
   a. wolf : pack
   b. elephant : jungle
   c. beagle : clan
   d. herd : peacock
   e. cow : farm

259. ODOMETER : DISTANCE
   a. scale : weight
   b. length : width
   c. inch : foot
   d. mileage : speed
   e. area : size

260. SIAMESE : CAT
   a. type : breed
   b. dog : puppy
   c. mark : spot
   d. romaine : lettuce
   e. collar : leash

261. PEDAL : BICYCLE
   a. inch : yardstick
   b. walk : skip
   c. tire : automobile
   d. buckle : belt
   e. oar : canoe

262. PULSATE : THROB
   a. walk : run
   b. tired : sleep
   c. examine : scrutinize
   d. ballet : dancer
   e. find : lose

263. ELEPHANT : PACHYDERM
   a. mantis : rodent
   b. poodle : feline
   c. kangaroo : marsupial
   d. zebra : horse
   e. tuna : mollusk

264. DEPRESSED : SAD
   a. neat : considerate
   b. towering : cringing
   c. rapid : plodding
   d. progressive : regressive
   e. exhausted : tired

265. PSYCHOLOGIST : NEUROSIS
   a. ophthalmologist : cataract
   b. dermatologist : fracture
   c. infant : pediatrician
   d. rash : orthopedist
   e. oncologist : measles

266. BINDING : BOOK
  a. criminal : gang
  b. display : museum
  c. artist : carpenter
  d. nail : hammer
  e. frame : picture

267. EXPLORE : DISCOVER
  a. read : skim
  b. research : learn
  c. write : print
  d. think : relate
  e. sleep : wake

268. COTTON : BALE
  a. butter : churn
  b. wine : ferment
  c. grain : shock
  d. curd : cheese
  e. beef : steak

269. DIVISION : SECTION
  a. layer : tier
  b. tether : bundle
  c. chapter : verse
  d. riser : stage
  e. dais : speaker

270. PASTORAL : RURAL
  a. metropolitan : urban
  b. harvest : autumn
  c. agrarian : benevolent
  d. sleepy : nocturnal
  e. wild : agricultural

271. WAITRESS : RESTAURANT
  a. doctor : diagnosis
  b. actor : role
  c. driver : truck
  d. teacher : school
  e. author : book

272. FINCH : BIRD
  a. frog : toad
  b. elephant : reptile
  c. Dalmatian : dog
  d. collie : marsupial
  e. ant : ladybug

273. RAIN : DRIZZLE
  a. swim : dive
  b. hop : shuffle
  c. juggle : bounce
  d. walk : run
  e. run : jog

274. SKEIN : YARN
  a. squeeze : lemon
  b. fire : coal
  c. ream : paper
  d. tree : lumber
  e. plow : acre

275. TAILOR : SUIT
  a. scheme : agent
  b. edit : manuscript
  c. revise : writer
  d. mention : opinion
  e. implode : building

► **Set 17** (Answers begin on page 119.)

Now try this last set of analogies, which are somewhat more difficult than the previous set. Remember that the first step in solving an analogy is to make up a sentence that describes the relationship between the first two words. Sometimes, your sentence may fit more than one answer choice. In these cases, be prepared to revise your original sentence. Each of the following questions consists of a related pair of words, followed by five pairs of words labeled **a** through **e**. Choose the pair that best represents a similar relationship to the one expressed in the original pair of words.

276. CONDUCTOR : ORCHESTRA
   a. jockey : mount
   b. thrasher : hay
   c. driver : tractor
   d. skipper : crew
   e. painter : house

277. JAUNDICE : LIVER
   a. rash : skin
   b. dialysis : kidney
   c. smog : lung
   d. valentine : heart
   e. imagination : brain

278. COBBLER : SHOE
   a. jockey : horse
   b. contractor : building
   c. mason : stone
   d. cowboy : boot
   e. potter : paint

279. PHOBIC : FEARFUL
   a. finicky : thoughtful
   b. cautious : emotional
   c. envious : desiring
   d. shy : familiar
   e. asinine : silly

280. INTEREST : OBSESSION
   a. mood : feeling
   b. weeping : sadness
   c. dream : fantasy
   d. plan : negation
   e. highlight : indication

281. MONK : DEVOTION
   a. maniac : pacifism
   b. explorer : contentment
   c. visionary : complacency
   d. rover : wanderlust
   e. philistine : culture

282. SLAPSTICK : LAUGHTER
   a. fallacy : dismay
   b. genre : mystery
   c. satire : anger
   d. mimicry : tears
   e. horror : fear

283. VERVE : ENTHUSIASM
   a. loyalty : duplicity
   b. devotion : reverence
   c. intensity : color
   d. eminence : anonymity
   e. generosity : elation

284. SOUND : CACOPHONY
   a. taste : style
   b. touch : massage
   c. smell : stench
   d. sight : panorama
   e. speech : oration

285. CONVICTION : INCARCERATION
   a. reduction : diminution
   b. induction : amelioration
   c. radicalization : estimation
   d. marginalization : intimidation
   e. proliferation : alliteration

286. DELTOID : MUSCLE
   a. radius : bone
   b. brain : nerve
   c. tissue : organ
   d. blood : vein
   e. scalpel : incision

287. UMBRAGE : OFFENSE
   a. confusion : penance
   b. infinity : meaning
   c. decorum : decoration
   d. elation : jubilance
   e. outrage : consideration

288. PROFESSOR : ERUDITE
   a. aviator : licensed
   b. inventor : imaginative
   c. procrastinator : conscientious
   d. overseer : wealthy
   e. moderator : vicious

289. DEPENDABLE : CAPRICIOUS
   a. fallible : cantankerous
   b. erasable : obtuse
   c. malleable : limpid
   d. capable : inept
   e. incorrigible : guilty

290. FROND : PALM
   a. quill : porcupine
   b. blade : evergreen
   c. scale : wallaby
   d. tusk : alligator
   e. blade : fern

291. METAPHOR : SYMBOL
   a. pentameter : poem
   b. rhythm : melody
   c. nuance : song
   d. slang : usage
   e. analogy : comparison

292. DIRGE : FUNERAL
   a. chain : letter
   b. bell : church
   c. telephone : call
   d. jingle : commercial
   e. hymn : concerto

293. FERAL : TAME
   a. rancid : rational
   b. repetitive : recurrent
   c. nettlesome : annoying
   d. repentant : honorable
   e. ephemeral : immortal

294. SPY : CLANDESTINE
   a. accountant : meticulous
   b. furrier : rambunctious
   c. lawyer : ironic
   d. shepherd : garrulous
   e. astronaut : opulent

295. DOMINANCE : HEGEMONY
   a. romance : sympathy
   b. furtherance : melancholy
   c. independence : autonomy
   d. tolerance : philanthropy
   e. recompense : hilarity

296. AERIE : EAGLE
   a. capital : government
   b. bridge : architect
   c. unit : apartment
   d. kennel : veterinarian
   e. house : person

▶ **Set 18** (Answers begin on page 120.)

Now try some reasoning questions that ask you to translate English words into an artificial language. First, you will be given a list of three "nonsense" words and their English word meanings. The question(s) that follow will ask you to reverse the process and translate an English word into the artificial language.

Your best approach to this type of question is to look for elements (parts) of the "nonsense" words that repeat. This is the best way to translate from the imaginary language to English. For example, if you know that *linsmerk* means oak tree and *linsdennel* means oak table, then you know that *lins* means oak. And, if *lins* means oak, *merk* must mean tree, and *dennel* must mean table. When you discover what a word element means in English, write it down. Then, look for the word elements that appear both on the list and in the answer choices.

297. Here are some words translated from an artificial language.
granamelke means big tree
pinimelke means little tree
melkehoon means tree house

Which word could mean "big house"?
a. granahoon
b. pinishur
c. pinihoon
d. melkegrana

298. Here are some words translated from an artificial language.
lelibroon means yellow hat
plekafroti means flower garden
frotimix means garden salad

Which word could mean "yellow flower"?
a. lelifroti
b. lelipleka
c. plekabroon
d. frotibroon

299. Here are some words translated from an artificial language.
moolokarn means blue sky
wilkospadi means bicycle race
moolowilko means blue bicycle

Which word could mean "racecar"?
a. wilkozwet
b. spadiwilko
c. moolobreil
d. spadivolo

300. Here are some words translated from an artificial language.
daftafoni means advisement
imodafta means misadvise
imolokti means misconduct

Which word could mean "statement"?
a. kratafoni
b. kratadafta
c. loktifoni
d. daftaimo

301. Here are some words translated from an artificial language.
dionot means oak tree
blyonot means oak leaf
blycrin means maple leaf

Which word could mean "maple syrup"?
a. blymuth
b. hupponot
c. patricrin
d. crinweel

302. Here are some words translated from an artificial language.

agnoscrenia means poisonous spider
delanocrenia means poisonous snake
agnosdeery means brown spider

Which word could mean "black widow spider"?
a. deeryclostagnos
b. agnosdelano
c. agnosvitriblunin
d. trymuttiagnos

303. Here are some words translated from an artificial language.

myncabel means saddle horse
conowir means trail ride
cabelalma means horse blanket

Which word could mean "horse ride"?
a. cabelwir
b. conocabel
c. almamyn
d. conoalma

304. Here are some words translated from an artificial language.

godabim means kidney stones
romzbim means kidney beans
romzbako means wax beans

Which word could mean "wax statue"?
a. godaromz
b. lazbim
c. wasibako
d. romzpeo

305. Here are some words translated from an artificial language.

tamceno means sky blue
cenorax means blue cheese
aplmitl means star bright

Which word could mean "bright sky"?
a. cenotam
b. mitltam
c. raxmitl
d. aplceno

306. Here are some words translated from an artificial language.

gorblflur means fan belt
pixngorbl means ceiling fan
arthtusl means tile roof

Which word could mean "ceiling tile"?
a. gorbltusl
b. flurgorbl
c. arthflur
d. pixnarth

307. Here are some words translated from an artificial language.

hapllesh means cloudburst
srenchoch means pinball
resbosrench means ninepin

Which word could mean "cloud nine"?
a. leshsrench
b. ochhapl
c. haploch
d. haplresbo

308. Here are some words translated from an artificial language.

migenlasan means cupboard
lasanpoen means boardwalk
cuopdansa means pullman

Which word could mean "walkway"?
a. poenmigen
b. cuopeisel
c. lasandansa
d. poenforc

▶ **Set 19** (Answers begin on page 121.)

Here is another set of questions that ask you to translate from an imaginary language into English. Remember, the best way to approach these questions is to translate each word element. When you discover what a word element means in English, write it down. Then, look for the word elements that appear both on the list and in the answer choices.

309. Here are some words translated from an artificial language.
morpirquat means birdhouse
beelmorpir means bluebird
beelclak means bluebell

Which word could mean "houseguest"?
a. morpirhunde
b. beelmoki
c. quathunde
d. clakquat

310. Here are some words translated from an artificial language.
slar means jump
slary means jumping
slarend means jumped

Which word could mean "playing"?
a. clargslarend
b. clargy
c. ellaclarg
d. slarmont

311. Here are some words translated from an artificial language.
briftamint means militant
uftonel means occupied
uftonalene means occupation

Which word could mean "occupant"?
a. elbrifta
b. uftonamint
c. elamint
d. briftalene

312. Here are some words translated from an artificial language.
krekinblaf means workforce
dritakrekin means groundwork
krekinalti means workplace

Which word could mean "someplace"?
a. moropalti
b. krekindrita
c. altiblaf
d. dritaalti

313. Here are some words translated from an artificial language.
plekapaki means fruitcake
pakishillen means cakewalk
treftalan means buttercup

Which word could mean "cupcake"?
a. shillenalan
b. treftpleka
c. pakitreft
d. alanpaki

314. Here are some words translated from an artificial language.
peslligen means basketball court
ligenstrisi means courtroom
oltaganti means placement test

Which word could mean "guest room"?
a. peslstrisi
b. vosefstrisi
c. gantipesl
d. oltastrisi

315. Here are some words translated from an artificial language.

jalkamofti means happy birthday
moftihoze means birthday party
mentogunn means goodness

Which word could mean "happiness"?
a. jalkagunn
b. mentohoze
c. moftihoze
d. hozemento

316. Here are some words translated from an artificial language.

mallonpiml means blue light
mallontifl means blueberry
arpantifl means raspberry

Which word could mean "lighthouse"?
a. tiflmallon
b. pimlarpan
c. mallonarpan
d. pimldoken

317. Here are some words translated from an artificial language.

gemolinea means fair warning
gerimitu means report card
gilageri means weather report

Which word could mean "fair weather?"
a. gemogila
b. gerigeme
c. gemomitu
d. gerimita

318. Here are some words translated from an artificial language.

aptaose means first base
eptaose means second base
lartabuk means ballpark

Which word could mean "baseball"?
a. buklarta
b. oseepta
c. bukose
d. oselarta

319. Here are some words translated from an artificial language.

relftaga means carefree
otaga means careful
fertaga means careless

Which word could mean "aftercare"?
a. zentaga
b. tagafer
c. tagazen
d. relffer

320. Here are some words translated from an artificial language.

malgauper means peach cobbler
malgaport means peach juice
moggagrop means apple jelly

Which word could mean "apple juice"?
a. moggaport
b. malgaauper
c. gropport
d. moggagrop

▶ **Set 20** (Answers begin on page 122.)

The questions in this set ask you to match definitions to particular situations. For each question, you will be given a definition and four possible answer choices. Read each definition and all four choices carefully, and find the answer that provides the best example of the given definition. Answer each question *solely* on the basis of the definition given.

321. **Violating an Apartment Lease** occurs when a tenant does something prohibited by the legally binding document that he or she has signed with a landlord. Which situation below is the best example of Violating an Apartment Lease?

   a. Tim has decided to move to another city, so he calls his landlord to tell him that he is not interested in renewing his lease when it expires next month.

   b. Valerie recently lost her job and, for the last three months, has neglected to pay her landlord the monthly rent they agreed upon in writing when she moved into her apartment eight months ago.

   c. Mark writes a letter to his landlord that lists numerous complaints about the apartment he has agreed to rent for two years.

   d. Leslie thinks that her landlord is neglecting the building in which she rents an apartment. She calls her attorney to ask for advice.

322. It is appropriate to compensate someone if you have damaged his or her property in some way. This is called **Restitution**. Which situation below is the best example of Restitution?

   a. Jake borrows Leslie's camera and the lens shatters when it falls on the ground because he fails to zipper the case. When Jake returns the camera, he tells Leslie that he will pay for the repair.

   b. Rebecca borrows her neighbor's car, and when she returns it, the gas tank is practically empty. She apologizes profusely and tells her neighbor she will be more considerate the next time.

   c. Aaron asks Tom to check in on his apartment while he is out of town. When Tom arrives, he discovers that a pipe has burst and there is a considerable amount of water damage. He calls a plumber to repair the pipe.

   d. Lisa suspects that the pothole in her company's parking lot caused her flat tire. She tells her boss that she thinks the company should pay for the repair.

323. People **speculate** when they consider a situation and assume something to be true based on inconclusive evidence. Which situation below is the best example of Speculation?

   a. Francine decides that it would be appropriate to wear jeans to her new office on Friday after reading about "Casual Fridays" in her employee handbook.

   b. Mary spends thirty minutes sitting in traffic and wishes that she took the train instead of driving.

   c. After consulting several guidebooks and her travel agent, Jennifer feels confident that the hotel she has chosen is first-rate.

   d. When Emily opens the door in tears, Theo guesses that she's had a death in her family.

324. A **Guarantee** is a promise or assurance that attests to the quality of a product that is either (1) given in writing by the manufacturer or (2) given verbally by the person selling the product. Which situation below is the best example of a Guarantee?

a. Melissa purchases a DVD player with the highest consumer ratings in its category.

b. The salesperson advises Curt to be sure that he buys an air conditioner with a guarantee.

c. The local auto body shop specializes in refurbishing and selling used cars.

d. Lori buys a used digital camera from her coworker who says that she will refund Lori's money if the camera's performance is not of the highest quality.

325. **Reentry** occurs when a person leaves his or her social system for a period of time and then returns. Which situation below best describes Reentry?

a. When he is offered a better paying position, Jacob leaves the restaurant he manages to manage a new restaurant on the other side of town.

b. Catherine is spending her junior year of college studying abroad in France.

c. Malcolm is readjusting to civilian life after two years of overseas military service.

d. After several miserable months, Sharon decides that she can no longer share an apartment with her roommate Hilary.

326. **Embellishing the Truth** occurs when a person adds fictitious details or exaggerates facts or true stories. Which situation below is the best example of Embellishing the Truth?

a. Isabel goes to the theater, and the next day, she tells her coworkers she thought the play was excellent.

b. The realtor describes the house, which is eleven blocks away from the ocean, as prime waterfront property.

c. During the job interview, Fred, who has been teaching elementary school for ten years, describes himself as a very experienced teacher.

d. The basketball coach says it is likely that only the most talented players will get a college scholarship.

327. **Applying for Seasonal Employment** occurs when a person requests to be considered for a job that is dependent on a particular season or time of year. Which situation below is the best example of Applying for Seasonal Employment?

a. The ski instructors at Top of the Peak Ski School work from December through March.

b. Matthew prefers jobs that allow him to work outdoors.

c. Lucinda makes an appointment with the beach resort restaurant manager to interview for the summer waitressing position that was advertised in the newspaper.

d. Doug's ice cream shop stays open until 11 P.M. during the summer months.

328. An **Informal Gathering** occurs when a group of people get together in a casual, relaxed manner. Which situation below is the best example of an Informal Gathering?
  a. The book club meets on the first Thursday evening of every month.
  b. After finding out about his promotion, Jeremy and a few coworkers decide to go out for a quick drink after work.
  c. Mary sends out 25 invitations for the bridal shower she is giving for her sister.
  d. Whenever she eats at the Mexican restaurant, Clara seems to run into Peter.

329. The rules of baseball state that a batter **Legally Completes His Time at Bat** when he is put out or becomes a base runner. Which situation below is the best example of a batter Legally Completing His Time at Bat?
  a. Jared's blooper over the head of the shortstop puts him in scoring position.
  b. The umpire calls a strike, even though the last pitch was way outside.
  c. The pitcher throws his famous knuckleball, Joe swings and misses, and the umpire calls a strike.
  d. The count is two balls and two strikes as Mario waits for the next pitch.

330. In the Maple Hill school district, a **Five-Day Suspension** occurs when a student is not permitted to attend school for five days for (1) physically assaulting another student, a teacher, or a school employee or (2) willfully destructing or defacing school property. Which situation below is the best example of a Five-Day Suspension?
  a. Lillian gets caught cheating on a math test for the second time and is suspended from school.
  b. Marc is asked to leave the classroom due to his constant disruptions.
  c. Franny uses spray paint to write derogatory comments on the locker room wall and she is given a suspension.
  d. Ms. Farmer tells her class that students who fail the midterm exam will be expected to stay after school for tutoring help.

331. A **Tiebreaker** is an additional contest or period of play designed to establish a winner among tied contestants. Which situation below is the best example of a Tiebreaker?
  a. At halftime, the score is tied at 28.
  b. Mary and Megan have each scored three goals in the game.
  c. The referee tosses a coin to decide which team will have possession of the ball first.
  d. The Sharks and the Bears each finished with 14 points, and they are now battling it out in a five-minute overtime.

341. Mrs. Carson took a taxi to meet her three friends for lunch. They were waiting for her outside the restaurant when she pulled up in the car. She was so excited to see her friends that she left her tote bag in the taxi. As the taxi pulled away, she and her friends took notice of the license plate number so they would be able to identify the car when they called the taxi company. The four license plate numbers below represent what each of the four women thinks she saw. Which one is most likely the license plate number of the taxi?
a. JXK 12L
b. JYK 12L
c. JXK 12I
d. JXX 12L

342. Zachary has invited his three buddies over to watch the basketball game on his wide-screen television. They are all hungry, but no one wants to leave to get food. Just as they are arguing about who should make the food run, a commercial comes on for a local pizzeria that delivers. The phone number flashes on the screen briefly and they all try to remember it. By the time Zachary grabs a pen and paper, each of them recollects a different number. Which of the numbers is most likely the telephone number of the pizzeria?
a. 995-9266
b. 995-9336
c. 995-9268
d. 995-8266

Answer question 343 solely on the basis of the following information.

When a new employee is hired at the law firm, a human resources representative should take the following steps on the employee's first day of work.

1. Greet the employee in the reception area and offer him coffee or tea.

2. Take the employee back to the human resources office and have him complete a general information questionnaire, a healthcare insurance form, and a tax form.
3. Take a photograph of the employee for his identification card.
4. Issue the employee a temporary identification card.
5. Walk the employee to the department in which he will be working and introduce him to his colleagues.
6. Bring the employee to his office or cubicle.

343. It is Kate Milford's first day of work as a paralegal at the law firm of Jasper, Jenkins & Mead. Taylor Franklin, the human resources manager, greets Kate in the reception area and gets her a cup of tea as they walk back to the human resources office. Taylor asks Kate to sit at a table and fill out three forms. While Kate completes the forms, Taylor checks her messages and asks her secretary to confirm a meeting she has for later that morning. Taylor then takes a photograph of Kate that will be used on her company identification card. As Taylor walks Kate over to the paralegal department, she tells her that the identification card should be ready in a couple of days. Taylor introduces Kate to her new colleagues, who all greet her quite warmly, and then shows her to her new cubicle, jots down her phone extension, and says that Kate should call her if she has any questions at all. Taylor Franklin's actions were
a. proper, because she is the human resources manager and knows how to greet a new employee.
b. improper, because she did not spend enough time making sure that Kate was comfortable.
c. proper, because she told Kate that she should feel free to call her if she had questions.
d. improper, because she did not issue a temporary identification card.

332. Establishing a Power of Attorney occurs when a legal document is created that gives one individual the authority to act for another. Which situation below is the best example of Establishing a Power of Attorney?
a. Louise is selling her house and she hires a lawyer to review the contract.
b. Simone's mother can no longer get to the bank to cash her checks and make deposits, so she has taken legal steps to enable Simone to do these things for her.
c. Jack's father is elderly and Jack thinks he is no longer able to make decisions for himself.
d. At her daughter's urging, Mrs. Lenox opens up a retirement account with the local bank.

333. Erratic Behavior occurs when an individual acts in a manner that lacks consistency, regularity, and uniformity. Which situation below is the best example of Erratic Behavior?
a. Julia cannot contain her anger whenever the subject of local politics is discussed.
b. Martin has just been told that he is being laid off. Before leaving his supervisor's office, he punches a hole in the door.
c. Rhonda has visited the dealership several times, but she still cannot decide which car to buy.
d. In the past month, Jeffrey, who has been a model employee for three years, has repeatedly called in sick, forgotten important meetings, and been verbally abusive to colleagues.

334. Posthumous Publication occurs when a book is published after the author's death. Which situation below is the best example of Posthumous Publication?
a. Richard's illness took his life before he was able to enjoy the amazing early reviews of his novel.
b. Melissa's publisher cancels her book contract after she fails to deliver the manuscript on time.
c. Clarence never thought he'd live to see the third book in his trilogy published.
d. Elizabeth is honored with a prestigious literary award for her writing career and her daughter accepts the award on behalf of her deceased mother.

► Set 21 (Answers begin on page 124.)

This set contains additional situations. Each question presents a situation and asks you to make a judgment regarding that particular circumstance. Answer each one *solely* on the basis of the information given.

335. The school principal has received complaints from parents about bullying in the school yard during recess. He wants to investigate and end this situation as soon as possible, so he has asked the recess aides to watch closely. Which situation should the recess aides report to the principal?
   a. A girl is sitting glumly on a bench reading a book and not interacting with her peers.
   b. Four girls are surrounding another girl and seem to have possession of her backpack.
   c. Two boys are playing a one-on-one game of basketball and are arguing over the last basket scored.
   d. Three boys are huddled over a handheld video game, which isn't supposed to be on school grounds.

336. Dr. Miller has a busy pediatric dentistry practice and she needs a skilled, reliable hygienist to keep things running smoothly. The last two people she hired were recommended by top dentists in the area, but they each lasted less than one month. She is now in desperate need of a hygienist who can competently handle the specific challenges of her practice. Which one of the following candidates should Dr. Miller consider most seriously?
   a. Marilyn has been a hygienist for fifteen years, and her current employer, who is about to retire, says she is the best in the business. The clientele she has worked with consists of some of the wealthiest and most powerful citizens in the county.
   b. Lindy recently graduated at the top of her class from one of the best dental hygiene programs in the state. Prior to becoming a dental hygienist, Lindy spent two years working in a day care center.
   c. James has worked as a dental hygienist for three years in a public health clinic. He is very interested in securing a position in a private dental office.
   d. Kathy is an experienced and highly recommended dental hygienist who is also finishing up a degree in early childhood education, which she hopes will get her a job as a preschool teacher. She is eager to find a job in a pediatric practice, since she has always wanted to work with children.

337. Mrs. Jansen recently moved to Arizona. She wants to fill her new backyard with flowering plants. Although she is an experienced gardener, she isn't very well-versed in what plants will do well in the Arizona climate. Also, there is a big tree in her backyard making for shady conditions and she isn't sure what plants will thrive without much direct sunlight. Her favorite gardening catalog offers several backyard seed packages. Which one should Mrs. Jansen choose?
   a. The Rainbow Collection is ideal for Northeast gardens. It includes a variety of colorful perennials that thrive in cool, moist conditions.
   b. The Greenhouse Collection will blossom year after year if planted in brightly lit locations and watered regularly.
   c. The Treehouse Collection will provide lush green plants with delicate colorful flowers that thrive in shady and partially shady locations.
   d. The Oasis Collection includes a variety of perennials that thrive in dry climates and bright sunlight.

338. Eileen is planning a special birthday dinner for her husband's 35th birthday. She wants the evening to be memorable, but her husband is a simple man who would rather be in jeans at a baseball game than in a suit at a fancy restaurant. Which restaurant below should Eileen choose?
   a. Alfredo's offers fine Italian cuisine and an elegant Tuscan décor. Patrons will feel as though they've spent the evening in a luxurious Italian villa.
   b. Pancho's Mexican Buffet is an all-you-can-eat family style smorgasbord with the best tacos in town.
   c. The Parisian Bistro is a four-star French restaurant where guests are treated like royalty. Chef Dilbert Olay is famous for his beef bourguignon.
   d. Marty's serves delicious, hearty meals in a charming setting reminiscent of a baseball clubhouse in honor of the owner, Marty Lester, a former major league baseball all-star.

339. Mark is working with a realtor to find a location for the toy store he plans to open in his town. He is looking for a place that is either in, or not too far from, the center of town and one that would attract the right kind of foot traffic. Which of the following locations should Mark's realtor call to his attention?
   a. a storefront in a new high-rise building near the train station in the center of town whose occupants are mainly young, childless professionals who use the train to commute to their offices each day
   b. a little shop three blocks away from the town's main street, located across the street from an elementary school and next door to an ice cream store
   c. a stand-alone storefront on a quiet residential street ten blocks away from the town's center
   d. a storefront in a small strip mall located on the outskirts of town that is also occupied by a pharmacy and a dry cleaner

340. Rita, an accomplished pastry chef who is well known for her artistic and exquisite wedding cakes, opened a bakery one year ago and is surprised that business has been so slow. A consultant she hired to conduct market research has reported that the local population doesn't think of her shop as one they would visit on a daily basis but rather a place they'd visit if they were celebrating a special occasion. Which of the following strategies should Rita employ to increase her daily business?
   a. making coupons available that entitle the coupon holder to receive a 25% discount on wedding, anniversary, or birthday cakes
   b. exhibiting at the next Bridal Expo and having pieces of one of her wedding cakes available for tasting
   c. placing a series of ads in the local newspaper that advertise the wide array of breads, muffins, and cookies offered at her shop
   d. moving the bakery to the other side of town

Answer question 344 solely on the basis of the following information.

When a client comes in looking for a new home, the real estate agency requires its realtors to follow some specific guidelines during the first meeting. The realtor is expected to do the following.

1. Be sure the client is comfortably seated and has been offered a drink.
2. Get background information on the client's current living circumstances.
3. Ask the client what qualities she is looking for in a house.
4. Discuss the price range that the client has in mind and determine whether or not she has been preapproved for a mortgage.
5. With the computer screen facing the client, browse the current house listings and print out information for any of the houses that the client would like to see in person.
6. Ask the client if she is available to look at some of the houses immediately, and if not, make an appointment to show her the houses as soon as possible.

344. Marcus and Cynthia Howard arrive at Smithfield Realty for their appointment with realtor Patricia Russo. Ms. Russo leads the couple to a comfortable sofa in her office and gets them both a cup of coffee. Ms. Russo asks Marcus and Cynthia what kind of house they are looking for and it becomes clear that they have very particular ideas. Most importantly, they are looking for a house that is in walking distance of the train station. They also want a newer house, preferably one built after 1970.

They must have four bedrooms and central air conditioning. A finished basement would be a welcome bonus. Ms. Russo discusses price range with her new clients, and before the discussion is finished, they hand her a letter from their mortgage company that indicates that they have been preapproved for a mortgage. Together, the three of them browse the listings on Ms. Russo's computer screen and information is printed out for four houses that the couple would like to see. Ms. Russo determines that Marcus and Cynthia are free for another few hours, so the three of them head to her car to begin looking at potential new homes. Based on the company guidelines, the actions taken by Ms. Russo were

a. improper, because she was only able to find four houses that Marcus and Cynthia wanted to see.
b. proper, because she obtained all the necessary information from the clients.
c. improper, because she failed to get any details about the client's current living circumstances.
d. proper, because she didn't try to persuade the clients to consider houses that didn't meet all of their criteria.

345. The film director wants an actress for the lead role of Lucy who perfectly fits the description that appears in the original screenplay. He is not willing to consider actresses who do not resemble the character as she is described in the screenplay, no matter how talented they are. The screenplay describes Lucy as an average-sized, forty-something redhead, with deep brown eyes, very fair skin, and a brilliant smile. The casting agent has four actresses in mind.

Actress #1 is a stunning red-haired beauty who is 5'9" and in her mid-twenties. Her eyes are brown and she has an olive complexion.

Actress #2 has red hair, big brown eyes, and a fair complexion. She is in her mid-forties and is 5'5".

Actress #3 is 5'4" and of medium build. She has red hair, brown eyes, and is in her early forties.

Actress #4 is a blue-eyed redhead in her early thirties. She's of very slight build and stands at 5'.

Which two actresses should the casting agent send to meet the director?
a. 1, 2
b. 2, 3
c. 1, 4
d. 2, 4

346. The neighborhood block association has received many complaints about people knocking on doors and soliciting money for an unknown charity organization even though door-to-door solicitation is prohibited by local laws. Three residents have provided descriptions of individuals who have come to their door asking for money.

Solicitor #1 is a white male, 20–25 years old, 5'9", 145 pounds, with very short brown hair. He was wearing a dark blue suit and carrying a brown leather briefcase.

Solicitor #2 is a white male, 25–30 years old, 6'2", 200 pounds, with a shaved-head. He was wearing a red T-shirt and jeans.

Solicitor #3 is a white male, approximately 23 years old, 5'10", slight build, with short brown hair. He was wearing a blue suit.

Three days after the block association meeting, a resident noticed a man knocking on doors in the neighborhood and phoned the police to report the illegal activity. This solicitor was described as follows:

Solicitor #4 is a white male, 22 years old, 140 pounds, about 5'10", with short brown hair. He was carrying a briefcase and wearing a dark suit.

Based on this description, which of the three solicitations was also likely carried out by Solicitor #4?
a. #1, #2, and #3
b. #1, but not #2 and #3
c. #1 and #3, but not #2
d. #1 and #2, but not #3

► **Set 22** (Answers begin on page 125.)

Here's another type of verbal reasoning question. For each item in this set, you will be given a short, informational paragraph and four answer choices. Look for the statement that *must be* true according to the given information. The best way to approach this problem is to read the answer choices in turn, going back each time to look for that exact information in the short passage.

For questions 347 through 357, find the statement that *must be* true according to the given information.

347. Erin is twelve years old. For three years, she has been asking her parents for a dog. Her parents have told her that they believe a dog would not be happy in an apartment, but they have given her permission to have a bird. Erin has not yet decided what kind of bird she would like to have.
  a. Erin's parents like birds better than they like dogs.
  b. Erin does not like birds.
  c. Erin and her parents live in an apartment.
  d. Erin and her parents would like to move.

348. Last summer, Mike spent two weeks at a summer camp. There, he went hiking, swimming, and canoeing. This summer, Mike looks forward to attending a two-week music camp, where he hopes to sing, dance, and learn to play the guitar.
  a. Mike's parents want him to learn to play the guitar.
  b. Mike prefers music to outdoor activities.
  c. Mike goes to some type of camp every summer.
  d. Mike likes to sing and dance.

349. The Pacific yew is an evergreen tree that grows in the Pacific Northwest. The Pacific yew has a fleshy, poisonous fruit. Recently, taxol, a substance found in the bark of the Pacific yew, was discovered to be a promising new anticancer drug.
  a. Taxol is poisonous when taken by healthy people.
  b. Taxol has cured people from various diseases.
  c. People should not eat the fruit of the Pacific yew.
  d. The Pacific yew was considered worthless until taxol was discovered.

350. On weekends, Mr. Sanchez spends many hours working in his vegetable and flower gardens. Mrs. Sanchez spends her free time reading and listening to classical music. Both Mr. Sanchez and Mrs. Sanchez like to cook.
  a. Mr. Sanchez enjoys planting and growing vegetables.
  b. Mr. Sanchez does not like classical music.
  c. Mrs. Sanchez cooks the vegetables that Mr. Sanchez grows.
  d. Mrs. Sanchez enjoys reading nineteenth-century novels.

351. Tim's commute never bothered him because there were always seats available on the train and he was able to spend his 40 minutes comfortably reading the newspaper or catching up on paperwork. Ever since the train schedule changed, the train has been extremely crowded, and by the time the doors open at his station, there isn't a seat to be found.
   a. Tim would be better off taking the bus to work.
   b. Tim's commute is less comfortable since the train schedule changed.
   c. Many commuters will complain about the new train schedule.
   d. Tim will likely look for a new job closer to home.

352. When they heard news of the hurricane, Maya and Julian decided to change their vacation plans. Instead of traveling to the island beach resort, they booked a room at a fancy new spa in the mountains. Their plans were a bit more expensive, but they'd heard wonderful things about the spa and they were relieved to find availability on such short notice.
   a. Maya and Julian take beach vacations every year.
   b. The spa is overpriced.
   c. It is usually necessary to book at least six months in advance at the spa.
   d. Maya and Julian decided to change their vacation plans because of the hurricane.

353. Seahorse populations have declined everywhere that seahorses are fished. During the past five years, seahorse populations have decreased by 50%. Last year, biologists met to discuss what might be done to reverse this trend.
   a. Seahorses are likely to become extinct within five years.
   b. One way to increase seahorse populations is to ban the fishing of seahorses.
   c. Biologists from all over the world are working to save the seahorses.
   d. Seahorse fishermen have spoken out against the biologists.

354. Vincent has a paper route. Each morning, he delivers 37 newspapers to customers in his neighborhood. It takes Vincent 50 minutes to deliver all the papers. If Vincent is sick or has other plans, his friend Thomas, who lives on the same street, will sometimes deliver the papers for him.
   a. Vincent and Thomas live in the same neighborhood.
   b. It takes Thomas more than 50 minutes to deliver the papers.
   c. It is dark outside when Vincent begins his deliveries.
   d. Thomas would like to have his own paper route.

355. Georgia is older than her cousin Marsha. Marsha's brother Bart is older than Georgia. When Marsha and Bart are visiting with Georgia, all three like to play a game of Monopoly. Marsha wins more often than Georgia does.
   a. When he plays Monopoly with Marsha and Georgia, Bart often loses.
   b. Of the three, Georgia is the oldest.
   c. Georgia hates to lose at Monopoly.
   d. Of the three, Marsha is the youngest.

356. Ten new television shows appeared during the month of September. Five of the shows were sitcoms, three were hour-long dramas, and two were news-magazine shows. By January, only seven of these new shows were still on the air. Five of the shows that remained were sitcoms.

a. Only one of the news-magazine shows remained on the air.

b. Only one of the hour-long dramas remained on the air.

c. At least one of the shows that was cancelled was an hour-long drama.

d. Television viewers prefer sitcoms over hour-long dramas.

357. Sara lives in a large city on the East Coast. Her younger cousin Marlee lives in the Midwest in a small town with fewer than 1,000 residents. Marlee has visited Sara several times during the past five years. In the same period of time, Sara has visited Marlee only once.

a. Marlee likes Sara better than Sara likes Marlee.

b. Sara thinks small towns are boring.

c. Sara is older than Marlee.

d. Marlee wants to move to the East Coast.

▶ **Set 23** (Answers begin on page 126.)

The next three sets contain short logic problems. Each problem consists of three statements. Based on the first two statements, the third statement may be true, false, or uncertain.

Logic problems may appear daunting at first. However, solving these problems can be done in the most straightforward way. Simply translate the abstract relationships in the questions into real-world relationships, so you can see the facts more clearly. For example, if the problem is comparing the ages of three people, make a chart and list the names of the people and their possible ages according to the information given. Or, create a diagram using symbols to represent phrases like "older than" or "greater than."

358. Tanya is older than Eric.

Cliff is older than Tanya.

Eric is older than Cliff.

If the first two statements are true, the third statement is
a. true.
b. false.
c. uncertain.

359. During the past year, Josh saw more movies than Stephen.

Stephen saw fewer movies than Darren.

Darren saw more movies than Josh.

If the first two statements are true, the third statement is
a. true.
b. false.
c. uncertain.

360. All the tulips in Zoe's garden are white.

All the pansies in Zoe's garden are yellow.

All the flowers in Zoe's garden are either white or yellow.

If the first two statements are true, the third statement is
a. true.
b. false.
c. uncertain.

361. Blueberries cost more than strawberries.

Blueberries cost lest than raspberries.

Raspberries cost more than both strawberries and blueberries.

If the first two statements are true, the third statement is
a. true.
b. false.
c. uncertain.

362. All the offices on the 9th floor have wall-to-wall carpeting.

No wall-to-wall carpeting is pink.

None of the offices on the 9th floor has pink wall-to-wall carpeting.

If the first two statements are true, the third statement is
a. true.
b. false.
c. uncertain.

363. Class A has a higher enrollment than Class B.

Class C has a lower enrollment than Class B.

Class A has a lower enrollment than Class C.

If the first two statements are true, the third statement is
a. true.
b. false.
c. uncertain.

332. Establishing a Power of Attorney occurs when a legal document is created that gives one individual the authority to act for another. Which situation below is the best example of Establishing a Power of Attorney?
a. Louise is selling her house and she hires a lawyer to review the contract.
b. Simone's mother can no longer get to the bank to cash her checks and make deposits, so she has taken legal steps to enable Simone to do these things for her.
c. Jack's father is elderly and Jack thinks he is no longer able to make decisions for himself.
d. At her daughter's urging, Mrs. Lenox opens up a retirement account with the local bank.

333. Erratic Behavior occurs when an individual acts in a manner that lacks consistency, regularity, and uniformity. Which situation below is the best example of Erratic Behavior?
a. Julia cannot contain her anger whenever the subject of local politics is discussed.
b. Martin has just been told that he is being laid off. Before leaving his supervisor's office, he punches a hole in the door.
c. Rhonda has visited the dealership several times, but she still cannot decide which car to buy.
d. In the past month, Jeffrey, who has been a model employee for three years, has repeatedly called in sick, forgotten important meetings, and been verbally abusive to colleagues.

334. Posthumous Publication occurs when a book is published after the author's death. Which situation below is the best example of Posthumous Publication?
a. Richard's illness took his life before he was able to enjoy the amazing early reviews of his novel.
b. Melissa's publisher cancels her book contract after she fails to deliver the manuscript on time.
c. Clarence never thought he'd live to see the third book in his trilogy published.
d. Elizabeth is honored with a prestigious literary award for her writing career and her daughter accepts the award on behalf of her deceased mother.

► **Set 21** (Answers begin on page 124.)

This set contains additional situations. Each question presents a situation and asks you to make a judgment regarding that particular circumstance. Answer each one *solely* on the basis of the information given.

335. The school principal has received complaints from parents about bullying in the school yard during recess. He wants to investigate and end this situation as soon as possible, so he has asked the recess aides to watch closely. Which situation should the recess aides report to the principal?
   a. A girl is sitting glumly on a bench reading a book and not interacting with her peers.
   b. Four girls are surrounding another girl and seem to have possession of her backpack.
   c. Two boys are playing a one-on-one game of basketball and are arguing over the last basket scored.
   d. Three boys are huddled over a handheld video game, which isn't supposed to be on school grounds.

336. Dr. Miller has a busy pediatric dentistry practice and she needs a skilled, reliable hygienist to keep things running smoothly. The last two people she hired were recommended by top dentists in the area, but they each lasted less than one month. She is now in desperate need of a hygienist who can competently handle the specific challenges of her practice. Which one of the following candidates should Dr. Miller consider most seriously?
   a. Marilyn has been a hygienist for fifteen years, and her current employer, who is about to retire, says she is the best in the business. The clientele she has worked with

consists of some of the wealthiest and most powerful citizens in the county.
   b. Lindy recently graduated at the top of her class from one of the best dental hygiene programs in the state. Prior to becoming a dental hygienist, Lindy spent two years working in a day care center.
   c. James has worked as a dental hygienist for three years in a public health clinic. He is very interested in securing a position in a private dental office.
   d. Kathy is an experienced and highly recommended dental hygienist who is also finishing up a degree in early childhood education, which she hopes will get her a job as a preschool teacher. She is eager to find a job in a pediatric practice, since she has always wanted to work with children.

337. Mrs. Jansen recently moved to Arizona. She wants to fill her new backyard with flowering plants. Although she is an experienced gardener, she isn't very well-versed in what plants will do well in the Arizona climate. Also, there is a big tree in her backyard making for shady conditions and she isn't sure what plants will thrive without much direct sunlight. Her favorite gardening catalog offers several backyard seed packages. Which one should Mrs. Jansen choose?
   a. The Rainbow Collection is ideal for Northeast gardens. It includes a variety of colorful perennials that thrive in cool, moist conditions.
   b. The Greenhouse Collection will blossom year after year if planted in brightly lit locations and watered regularly.
   c. The Treehouse Collection will provide lush green plants with delicate colorful flowers

that thrive in shady and partially shady locations.

d. The Oasis Collection includes a variety of perennials that thrive in dry climates and bright sunlight.

338. Eileen is planning a special birthday dinner for her husband's 35th birthday. She wants the evening to be memorable, but her husband is a simple man who would rather be in jeans at a baseball game than in a suit at a fancy restaurant. Which restaurant below should Eileen choose?

a. Alfredo's offers fine Italian cuisine and an elegant Tuscan décor. Patrons will feel as though they've spent the evening in a luxurious Italian villa.

b. Pancho's Mexican Buffet is an all-you-can-eat family style smorgasbord with the best tacos in town.

c. The Parisian Bistro is a four-star French restaurant where guests are treated like royalty. Chef Dilbert Olay is famous for his beef bourguignon.

d. Marty's serves delicious, hearty meals in a charming setting reminiscent of a baseball clubhouse in honor of the owner, Marty Lester, a former major league baseball all-star.

339. Mark is working with a realtor to find a location for the toy store he plans to open in his town. He is looking for a place that is either in, or not too far from, the center of town and one that would attract the right kind of foot traffic. Which of the following locations should Mark's realtor call to his attention?

a. a storefront in a new high-rise building near the train station in the center of town whose occupants are mainly young, child-

less professionals who use the train to commute to their offices each day

b. a little shop three blocks away from the town's main street, located across the street from an elementary school and next door to an ice cream store

c. a stand-alone storefront on a quiet residential street ten blocks away from the town's center

d. a storefront in a small strip mall located on the outskirts of town that is also occupied by a pharmacy and a dry cleaner

340. Rita, an accomplished pastry chef who is well known for her artistic and exquisite wedding cakes, opened a bakery one year ago and is surprised that business has been so slow. A consultant she hired to conduct market research has reported that the local population doesn't think of her shop as one they would visit on a daily basis but rather a place they'd visit if they were celebrating a special occasion. Which of the following strategies should Rita employ to increase her daily business?

a. making coupons available that entitle the coupon holder to receive a 25% discount on wedding, anniversary, or birthday cakes

b. exhibiting at the next Bridal Expo and having pieces of one of her wedding cakes available for tasting

c. placing a series of ads in the local newspaper that advertise the wide array of breads, muffins, and cookies offered at her shop

d. moving the bakery to the other side of town

341. Mrs. Carson took a taxi to meet her three friends for lunch. They were waiting for her outside the restaurant when she pulled up in the car. She was so excited to see her friends that she left her tote bag in the taxi. As the taxi pulled away, she and her friends took notice of the license plate number so they would be able to identify the car when they called the taxi company. The four license plate numbers below represent what each of the four women thinks she saw. Which one is most likely the license plate number of the taxi?

   a. JXK 12L
   b. JYK 12L
   c. JXK 12I
   d. JXX 12L

342. Zachary has invited his three buddies over to watch the basketball game on his wide-screen television. They are all hungry, but no one wants to leave to get food. Just as they are arguing about who should make the food run, a commercial comes on for a local pizzeria that delivers. The phone number flashes on the screen briefly and they all try to remember it. By the time Zachary grabs a pen and paper, each of them recollects a different number. Which of the numbers is most likely the telephone number of the pizzeria?

   a. 995-9266
   b. 995-9336
   c. 995-9268
   d. 995-8266

Answer question 343 solely on the basis of the following information.

When a new employee is hired at the law firm, a human resources representative should take the following steps on the employee's first day of work.

1. Greet the employee in the reception area and offer him coffee or tea.

2. Take the employee back to the human resources office and have him complete a general information questionnaire, a healthcare insurance form, and a tax form.

3. Take a photograph of the employee for his identification card.

4. Issue the employee a temporary identification card.

5. Walk the employee to the department in which he will be working and introduce him to his colleagues.

6. Bring the employee to his office or cubicle.

343. It is Kate Milford's first day of work as a paralegal at the law firm of Jasper, Jenkins & Mead. Taylor Franklin, the human resources manager, greets Kate in the reception area and gets her a cup of tea as they walk back to the human resources office. Taylor asks Kate to sit at a table and fill out three forms. While Kate completes the forms, Taylor checks her messages and asks her secretary to confirm a meeting she has for later that morning. Taylor then takes a photograph of Kate that will be used on her company identification card. As Taylor walks Kate over to the paralegal department, she tells her that the identification card should be ready in a couple of days. Taylor introduces Kate to her new colleagues, who all greet her quite warmly, and then shows her to her new cubicle, jots down her phone extension, and says that Kate should call her if she has any questions at all. Taylor Franklin's actions were

   a. proper, because she is the human resources manager and knows how to greet a new employee.
   b. improper, because she did not spend enough time making sure that Kate was comfortable.
   c. proper, because she told Kate that she should feel free to call her if she had questions.
   d. improper, because she did not issue a temporary identification card.

Answer question 344 solely on the basis of the following information.

When a client comes in looking for a new home, the real estate agency requires its realtors to follow some specific guidelines during the first meeting. The realtor is expected to do the following.

1. Be sure the client is comfortably seated and has been offered a drink.
2. Get background information on the client's current living circumstances.
3. Ask the client what qualities she is looking for in a house.
4. Discuss the price range that the client has in mind and determine whether or not she has been preapproved for a mortgage.
5. With the computer screen facing the client, browse the current house listings and print out information for any of the houses that the client would like to see in person.
6. Ask the client if she is available to look at some of the houses immediately, and if not, make an appointment to show her the houses as soon as possible.

344. Marcus and Cynthia Howard arrive at Smithfield Realty for their appointment with realtor Patricia Russo. Ms. Russo leads the couple to a comfortable sofa in her office and gets them both a cup of coffee. Ms. Russo asks Marcus and Cynthia what kind of house they are looking for and it becomes clear that they have very particular ideas. Most importantly, they are looking for a house that is in walking distance of the train station. They also want a newer house, preferably one built after 1970.

They must have four bedrooms and central air conditioning. A finished basement would be a welcome bonus. Ms. Russo discusses price range with her new clients, and before the discussion is finished, they hand her a letter from their mortgage company that indicates that they have been preapproved for a mortgage. Together, the three of them browse the listings on Ms. Russo's computer screen and information is printed out for four houses that the couple would like to see. Ms. Russo determines that Marcus and Cynthia are free for another few hours, so the three of them head to her car to begin looking at potential new homes. Based on the company guidelines, the actions taken by Ms. Russo were

a. improper, because she was only able to find four houses that Marcus and Cynthia wanted to see.
b. proper, because she obtained all the necessary information from the clients.
c. improper, because she failed to get any details about the client's current living circumstances.
d. proper, because she didn't try to persuade the clients to consider houses that didn't meet all of their criteria.

345. The film director wants an actress for the lead role of Lucy who perfectly fits the description that appears in the original screenplay. He is not willing to consider actresses who do not resemble the character as she is described in the screenplay, no matter how talented they are. The screenplay describes Lucy as an average-sized, forty-something redhead, with deep brown eyes, very fair skin, and a brilliant smile. The casting agent has four actresses in mind.

Actress #1 is a stunning red-haired beauty who is 5'9" and in her mid-twenties. Her eyes are brown and she has an olive complexion.

Actress #2 has red hair, big brown eyes, and a fair complexion. She is in her mid-forties and is 5'5".

Actress #3 is 5'4" and of medium build. She has red hair, brown eyes, and is in her early forties.

Actress #4 is a blue-eyed redhead in her early thirties. She's of very slight build and stands at 5'.

Which two actresses should the casting agent send to meet the director?
a. 1, 2
b. 2, 3
c. 1, 4
d. 2, 4

346. The neighborhood block association has received many complaints about people knocking on doors and soliciting money for an unknown charity organization even though door-to-door solicitation is prohibited by local laws. Three residents have provided descriptions of individuals who have come to their door asking for money.

Solicitor #1 is a white male, 20–25 years old, 5'9", 145 pounds, with very short brown hair. He was wearing a dark blue suit and carrying a brown leather briefcase.

Solicitor #2 is a white male, 25–30 years old, 6'2", 200 pounds, with a shaved-head. He was wearing a red T-shirt and jeans.

Solicitor #3 is a white male, approximately 23 years old, 5'10", slight build, with short brown hair. He was wearing a blue suit.

Three days after the block association meeting, a resident noticed a man knocking on doors in the neighborhood and phoned the police to report the illegal activity. This solicitor was described as follows:

Solicitor #4 is a white male, 22 years old, 140 pounds, about 5'10", with short brown hair. He was carrying a briefcase and wearing a dark suit.

Based on this description, which of the three solicitations was also likely carried out by Solicitor #4?
a. #1, #2, and #3
b. #1, but not #2 and #3
c. #1 and #3, but not #2
d. #1 and #2, but not #3

▶ **Set 22** (Answers begin on page 125.)

Here's another type of verbal reasoning question. For each item in this set, you will be given a short, informational paragraph and four answer choices. Look for the statement that *must be* true according to the given information. The best way to approach this problem is to read the answer choices in turn, going back each time to look for that exact information in the short passage.

For questions 347 through 357, find the statement that *must be* true according to the given information.

347. Erin is twelve years old. For three years, she has been asking her parents for a dog. Her parents have told her that they believe a dog would not be happy in an apartment, but they have given her permission to have a bird. Erin has not yet decided what kind of bird she would like to have.
  a. Erin's parents like birds better than they like dogs.
  b. Erin does not like birds.
  c. Erin and her parents live in an apartment.
  d. Erin and her parents would like to move.

348. Last summer, Mike spent two weeks at a summer camp. There, he went hiking, swimming, and canoeing. This summer, Mike looks forward to attending a two-week music camp, where he hopes to sing, dance, and learn to play the guitar.
  a. Mike's parents want him to learn to play the guitar.
  b. Mike prefers music to outdoor activities.
  c. Mike goes to some type of camp every summer.
  d. Mike likes to sing and dance.

349. The Pacific yew is an evergreen tree that grows in the Pacific Northwest. The Pacific yew has a fleshy, poisonous fruit. Recently, taxol, a substance found in the bark of the Pacific yew, was discovered to be a promising new anticancer drug.
  a. Taxol is poisonous when taken by healthy people.
  b. Taxol has cured people from various diseases.
  c. People should not eat the fruit of the Pacific yew.
  d. The Pacific yew was considered worthless until taxol was discovered.

350. On weekends, Mr. Sanchez spends many hours working in his vegetable and flower gardens. Mrs. Sanchez spends her free time reading and listening to classical music. Both Mr. Sanchez and Mrs. Sanchez like to cook.
  a. Mr. Sanchez enjoys planting and growing vegetables.
  b. Mr. Sanchez does not like classical music.
  c. Mrs. Sanchez cooks the vegetables that Mr. Sanchez grows.
  d. Mrs. Sanchez enjoys reading nineteenth-century novels.

351. Tim's commute never bothered him because there were always seats available on the train and he was able to spend his 40 minutes comfortably reading the newspaper or catching up on paperwork. Ever since the train schedule changed, the train has been extremely crowded, and by the time the doors open at his station, there isn't a seat to be found.
  a. Tim would be better off taking the bus to work.
  b. Tim's commute is less comfortable since the train schedule changed.
  c. Many commuters will complain about the new train schedule.
  d. Tim will likely look for a new job closer to home.

352. When they heard news of the hurricane, Maya and Julian decided to change their vacation plans. Instead of traveling to the island beach resort, they booked a room at a fancy new spa in the mountains. Their plans were a bit more expensive, but they'd heard wonderful things about the spa and they were relieved to find availability on such short notice.
  a. Maya and Julian take beach vacations every year.
  b. The spa is overpriced.
  c. It is usually necessary to book at least six months in advance at the spa.
  d. Maya and Julian decided to change their vacation plans because of the hurricane.

353. Seahorse populations have declined everywhere that seahorses are fished. During the past five years, seahorse populations have decreased by 50%. Last year, biologists met to discuss what might be done to reverse this trend.
  a. Seahorses are likely to become extinct within five years.
  b. One way to increase seahorse populations is to ban the fishing of seahorses.
  c. Biologists from all over the world are working to save the seahorses.
  d. Seahorse fishermen have spoken out against the biologists.

354. Vincent has a paper route. Each morning, he delivers 37 newspapers to customers in his neighborhood. It takes Vincent 50 minutes to deliver all the papers. If Vincent is sick or has other plans, his friend Thomas, who lives on the same street, will sometimes deliver the papers for him.
  a. Vincent and Thomas live in the same neighborhood.
  b. It takes Thomas more than 50 minutes to deliver the papers.
  c. It is dark outside when Vincent begins his deliveries.
  d. Thomas would like to have his own paper route.

355. Georgia is older than her cousin Marsha. Marsha's brother Bart is older than Georgia. When Marsha and Bart are visiting with Georgia, all three like to play a game of Monopoly. Marsha wins more often than Georgia does.
  a. When he plays Monopoly with Marsha and Georgia, Bart often loses.
  b. Of the three, Georgia is the oldest.
  c. Georgia hates to lose at Monopoly.
  d. Of the three, Marsha is the youngest.

356. Ten new television shows appeared during the month of September. Five of the shows were sitcoms, three were hour-long dramas, and two were news-magazine shows. By January, only seven of these new shows were still on the air. Five of the shows that remained were sitcoms.

  a. Only one of the news-magazine shows remained on the air.

  b. Only one of the hour-long dramas remained on the air.

  c. At least one of the shows that was cancelled was an hour-long drama.

  d. Television viewers prefer sitcoms over hour-long dramas.

357. Sara lives in a large city on the East Coast. Her younger cousin Marlee lives in the Midwest in a small town with fewer than 1,000 residents. Marlee has visited Sara several times during the past five years. In the same period of time, Sara has visited Marlee only once.

  a. Marlee likes Sara better than Sara likes Marlee.

  b. Sara thinks small towns are boring.

  c. Sara is older than Marlee.

  d. Marlee wants to move to the East Coast.

▶ Set 23 (Answers begin on page 126.)

The next three sets contain short logic problems. Each problem consists of three statements. Based on the first two statements, the third statement may be true, false, or uncertain.

Logic problems may appear daunting at first. However, solving these problems can be done in the most straightforward way. Simply translate the abstract relationships in the questions into real-world relationships, so you can see the facts more clearly. For example, if the problem is comparing the ages of three people, make a chart and list the names of the people and their possible ages according to the information given. Or, create a diagram using symbols to represent phrases like "older than" or "greater than."

358. Tanya is older than Eric.

Cliff is older than Tanya.

Eric is older than Cliff.

If the first two statements are true, the third statement is
a. true.
b. false.
c. uncertain.

359. During the past year, Josh saw more movies than Stephen.

Stephen saw fewer movies than Darren.

Darren saw more movies than Josh.

If the first two statements are true, the third statement is
a. true.
b. false.
c. uncertain.

360. All the tulips in Zoe's garden are white.

All the pansies in Zoe's garden are yellow.

All the flowers in Zoe's garden are either white or yellow.

If the first two statements are true, the third statement is
a. true.
b. false.
c. uncertain.

361. Blueberries cost more than strawberries.

Blueberries cost lest than raspberries.

Raspberries cost more than both strawberries and blueberries.

If the first two statements are true, the third statement is
a. true.
b. false.
c. uncertain.

362. All the offices on the 9th floor have wall-to-wall carpeting.

No wall-to-wall carpeting is pink.

None of the offices on the 9th floor has pink wall-to-wall carpeting.

If the first two statements are true, the third statement is
a. true.
b. false.
c. uncertain.

363. Class A has a higher enrollment than Class B.

Class C has a lower enrollment than Class B.

Class A has a lower enrollment than Class C.

If the first two statements are true, the third statement is
a. true.
b. false.
c. uncertain.

364. Rover weighs less than Fido.

Rover weighs more than Boomer.

Of the three dogs, Boomer weighs the least.

If the first two statements are true, the third statement is
a. true.
b. false.
c. uncertain.

365. All the trees in the park are flowering trees.

Some of the trees in the park are dogwoods.

All dogwoods are flowering trees.

If the first two statements are true, the third statement is
a. true.
b. false.
c. uncertain.

366. Apartments in the Riverdale Manor cost less than apartments in The Gaslight Commons.

Apartments in the Livingston Gate cost more than apartments in the The Gaslight Commons.

Of the three apartment buildings, the Livingston Gate costs the most.

If the first two statements are true, the third statement is
a. true.
b. false.
c. uncertain.

367. The Kingston Mall has more stores than the Galleria.

The Four Corners Mall has fewer stores than the Galleria.

The Kingston Mall has more stores than the Four Corners Mall.

If the first two statements are true, the third statement is
a. true.
b. false.
c. uncertain.

368. Mara runs faster than Gail.

Lily runs faster than Mara.

Gail runs faster than Lily.

If the first two statements are true, the third statement is
a. true.
b. false.
c. uncertain.

► Set 24 (Answers begin on page 127.)

Some of the logic questions in this set ask you to determine the direction of a particular place in relation to other places. For these problems, instead of making a chart or grid, draw a very simple map and label North, South, East, and West to help you see where the places are located in relation to each other.

369. Oat cereal has more fiber than corn cereal but less fiber than bran cereal.

Corn cereal has more fiber than rice cereal but less fiber than wheat cereal.

Of the three kinds of cereal, rice cereal has the least amount of fiber.

If the first two statements are true, the third statement is
a. true.
b. false.
c. uncertain.

370. On the day the Barton triplets are born, Jenna weighs more than Jason.

Jason weighs less than Jasmine.

Of the three babies, Jasmine weighs the most.

If the first two statements are true, the third statement is
a. true.
b. false.
c. uncertain.

371. The temperature on Monday was lower than on Tuesday.

The temperature on Wednesday was lower than on Tuesday.

The temperature on Monday was higher than on Wednesday.

If the first two statements are true, the third statement is
a. true.
b. false.
c. uncertain.

372. Spot is bigger than King and smaller than Sugar.

Ralph is smaller than Sugar and bigger than Spot.

King is bigger than Ralph.

If the first two statements are true, the third statement is
a. true.
b. false.
c. uncertain.

373. A fruit basket contains more apples than lemons.

There are more lemons in the basket than there are oranges.

The basket contains more apples than oranges.

If the first two statements are true, the third statement is
a. true.
b. false.
c. uncertain.

374. The Shop and Save Grocery is south of Greenwood Pharmacy.

Rebecca's house is northeast of Greenwood Pharmacy.

Rebecca's house is west of the Shop and Save Grocery.

If the first two statements are true, the third statement is
a. true.
b. false.
c. uncertain.

375. Joe is younger than Kathy.

Mark was born after Joe.

Kathy is older than Mark.

If the first two statements are true, the third statement is
a. true.
b. false.
c. uncertain.

376. All spotted Gangles have long tails.

Short-haired Gangles always have short tails.

Long-tailed Gangles never have short hair.

If the first two statements are true, the third statement is
a. true.
b. false.
c. uncertain.

377. Battery X lasts longer than Battery Y.

Battery Y doesn't last as long as Battery Z.

Battery Z lasts longer than Battery X.

If the first two statements are true, the third statement is
a. true.
b. false.
c. uncertain.

378. Martina is sitting in the desk behind Jerome.

Jerome is sitting in the desk behind Bryant.

Bryant is sitting in the desk behind Martina.

If the first two statements are true, the third statement is
a. true.
b. false.
c. uncertain.

379. Middletown is north of Centerville.

Centerville is east of Penfield.

Penfield is northwest of Middletown.

If the first two statements are true, the third statement is
a. true.
b. false.
c. uncertain.

▶ **Set 25** (Answers begin on page 128.)

Here's your last set of "true-false-uncertain" problems. Remember, the best way to answer questions like this is usually to draw a quick diagram or take notes.

380. Taking the train across town is quicker than taking the bus.

Taking the bus across town is slower than driving a car.

Taking the train across town is quicker than driving a car.

If the first two statements are true, the third statement is
a. true.
b. false.
c. uncertain.

381. All Lamels are Signots with buttons.

No yellow Signots have buttons.

No Lamels are yellow.

If the first two statements are true, the third statement is
a. true.
b. false.
c. uncertain.

382. The hotel is two blocks east of the drugstore.

The market is one block west of the hotel.

The drugstore is west of the market.

If the first two statements are true, the third statement is
a. true.
b. false.
c. uncertain.

383. Tom puts on his socks before he puts on his shoes.

He puts on his shirt before he puts on his jacket.

Tom puts on his shoes before he puts on his shirt.

If the first two statements are true, the third statement is
a. true.
b. false.
c. uncertain.

384. Three pencils cost the same as two erasers.

Four erasers cost the same as one ruler.

Pencils are more expensive than rulers.

If the first two statements are true, the third statement is
a. true.
b. false.
c. uncertain.

385. A jar of jelly beans contains more red beans than green.

There are more yellow beans than red.

The jar contains fewer yellow jelly beans than green ones.

If the first two statements are true, the third statement is
a. true.
b. false.
c. uncertain.

386. Cloudy days tend to be more windy than sunny days.

Foggy days tend to be less windy than cloudy days.

Sunny days tend to be less windy than foggy days.

If the first two statements are true, the third statement is
a. true.
b. false.
c. uncertain.

387. The bookstore has a better selection of post-cards than the newsstand does.

The selection of postcards at the drugstore is better than at the bookstore.

The drugstore has a better selection of post-cards than the bookstore or the newsstand.

If the first two statements are true, the third statement is
a. true.
b. false.
c. uncertain.

388. At a parking lot, a sedan is parked to the right of a pickup and to the left of a sport utility vehicle.

A minivan is parked to the left of the pickup.

The minivan is parked between the pickup and the sedan.

If the first two statements are true, the third statement is
a. true.
b. false.
c. uncertain.

389. A toothpick is useful.

Useful things are valuable.

A toothpick is valuable.

If the first two statements are true, the third statement is
a. true.
b. false.
c. uncertain.

► **Set 26** (Answers begin on page 129.)

The logic problems in this set present you with three true statements: Fact 1, Fact 2, and Fact 3. Then, you are given three more statements (labeled I, II, and III), and you must determine which of these, if any, is also a fact. One or two of the statements could be true; all of the statements could be true; or none of the statements could be true. Choose your answer based *solely* on the information given in the first three facts.

390. Fact 1: Jessica has four children.

Fact 2: Two of the children have blue eyes and two of the children have brown eyes.

Fact 3: Half of the children are girls.

If the first three statements are facts, which of the following statements must also be a fact?

  I. At least one girl has blue eyes.

  II. Two of the children are boys.

 III. The boys have brown eyes.

a. II only

b. I and III only

c. II and III only

d. None of the statements is a known fact.

391. Fact 1: All hats have brims.

Fact 2: There are black hats and blue hats.

Fact 3: Baseball caps are hats.

If the first three statements are facts, which of the following statements must also be a fact?

  I. All caps have brims.

  II. Some baseball caps are blue.

 III. Baseball caps have no brims.

a. I only

b. II only

c. I, II, and III

d. None of the statements is a known fact.

392. Fact 1: All chickens are birds.

Fact 2: Some chickens are hens.

Fact 3: Female birds lay eggs.

If the first three statements are facts, which of the following statements must also be a fact?

  I. All birds lay eggs.

  II. Hens are birds.

 III. Some chickens are not hens.

a. II only

b. II and III only

c. I, II, and III

d. None of the statements is a known fact.

393. Fact 1: Most stuffed toys are stuffed with beans.

Fact 2: There are stuffed bears and stuffed tigers.

Fact 3: Some chairs are stuffed with beans.

If the first three statements are facts, which of the following statements must also be a fact?

  I. Only children's chairs are stuffed with beans.

  II. All stuffed tigers are stuffed with beans.

 III. Stuffed monkeys are not stuffed with beans.

a. I only

b. II only

c. II and III only

d. None of the statements is a known fact.

394. Fact 1: Pictures can tell a story.

Fact 2: All storybooks have pictures.

Fact 3: Some storybooks have words.

If the first three statements are facts, which of the following statements must also be a fact?

  I. Pictures can tell a story better than words can.

 II. The stories in storybooks are very simple.

III. Some storybooks have both words and pictures.

a. I only

b. II only

c. III only

d. None of the statements is a known fact.

395. Fact 1: Robert has four vehicles.

Fact 2: Two of the vehicles are red.

Fact 3: One of the vehicles is a minivan.

If the first three statements are facts, which of the following statements must also be a fact?

  I. Robert has a red minivan.

 II. Robert has three cars.

III. Robert's favorite color is red.

a. I only

b. II only

c. II and III only

d. None of the statements is a known fact.

396. Fact 1: Islands are surrounded by water.

Fact 2: Maui is an island.

Fact 3: Maui was formed by a volcano.

If the first three statements are facts, which of the following statements must also be a fact?

  I. Maui is surrounded by water.

 II. All islands are formed by volcanoes.

III. All volcanoes are on islands.

a. I only

b. III only

c. I and II only

d. None of the statements is a known fact.

397. Fact 1: All drink mixes are beverages.

Fact 2: All beverages are drinkable.

Fact 3: Some beverages are red.

If the first three statements are facts, which of the following statements must also be a fact?

  I. Some drink mixes are red.

 II. All beverages are drink mixes.

III. All red drink mixes are drinkable.

a. I only

b. II only

c. I and III

d. None of the statements is a known fact.

398. Fact 1: Eyeglass frames cost between $35 and $350.

Fact 2: Some eyeglass frames are made of titanium.

Fact 3: Some eyeglass frames are made of plastic.

If the first three statements are facts, which of the following statements must also be a fact?

  I. Titanium eyeglass frames cost more than plastic frames.

 II. Expensive eyeglass frames last longer than cheap frames.

III. Only a few eyeglass frames cost less than $35.

a. II only

b. I and II only

c. II and III only

d. None of the statements is a known fact.

399. Fact 1: Some pens don't write.

Fact 2: All blue pens write.

Fact 3: Some writing utensils are pens.

If the first three statements are facts, which of the following statements must also be a fact?

I. Some writing utensils don't write.

II. Some writing utensils are blue.

III. Some blue writing utensils don't write.

a. II only

b. I and II only

c. II and III only

d. None of the statements is a known fact.

400. Fact 1: Mary said, "Ann and I both have cats."

Fact 2: Ann said, "I don't have a cat."

Fact 3: Mary always tells the truth, but Ann sometimes lies.

If the first three statements are facts, which of the following statements must also be a fact?

I. Ann has a cat.

II. Mary has a cat.

III. Ann is lying.

a. II only

b. I and II only

c. I, II, and III

d. None of the statements is a known fact.

401. Fact 1: All dogs like to run.

Fact 2: Some dogs like to swim.

Fact 3: Some dogs look like their masters.

If the first three statements are facts, which of the following statements must also be a fact?

I. All dogs who like to swim look like their masters.

II. Dogs who like to swim also like to run.

III. Dogs who like to run do not look like their masters.

a. I only

b. II only

c. II and III only

d. None of the statements is a known fact.

► **Set 27** (Answers begin on page 130.)

Here is yet another set of logic questions. The logic problems in this set are somewhat more complex than the ones in the previous sets, but your approach should be the same. Make a chart or grid so that you can order the given information.

402. Children are in pursuit of a dog whose leash has broken. James is directly behind the dog. Ruby is behind James. Rachel is behind Ruby. Max is ahead of the dog walking down the street in the opposite direction. As the children and dog pass, Max turns around and joins the pursuit. He runs in behind Ruby. James runs faster and is alongside the dog on the left. Ruby runs faster and is alongside the dog on the right. Which child is directly behind the dog?
   a. James
   b. Ruby
   c. Rachel
   d. Max

403. Nurse Kemp has worked more night shifts in a row than Nurse Rogers, who has worked five. Nurse Miller has worked fifteen night shifts in a row, more than Nurses Kemp and Rogers combined. Nurse Calvin has worked eight night shifts in a row, less than Nurse Kemp. How many night shifts in a row has Nurse Kemp worked?
   a. eight
   b. nine
   c. ten
   d. eleven

404. Four friends in the sixth grade were sharing a pizza. They decided that the oldest friend would get the extra piece. Randy is two months older than Greg, who is three months younger than Ned. Kent is one month older than Greg. Who should get the extra piece of pizza?
   a. Randy
   b. Greg
   c. Ned
   d. Kent

405. A four-person crew from Classic Colors is painting Mr. Field's house. Michael is painting the front of the house. Ross is in the alley behind the house painting the back. Jed is painting the window frames on the north side, Shawn is on the south. If Michael switches places with Jed, and Jed then switches places with Shawn, where is Shawn?
   a. in the alley behind the house
   b. on the north side of the house
   c. in front of the house
   d. on the south side of the house

406. In a four-day period—Monday through Thursday—each of the following temporary office workers worked only one day, each a different day. Ms. Johnson was scheduled to work on Monday, but she traded with Mr. Carter, who was originally scheduled to work on Wednesday. Ms. Falk traded with Mr. Kirk, who was originally scheduled to work on Thursday. After all the switching was done, who worked on Tuesday?
   a. Mr. Carter
   b. Ms. Falk
   c. Ms. Johnson
   d. Mr. Kirk

407. The high school math department needs to appoint a new chairperson, which will be based on seniority. Ms. West has less seniority than Mr. Temple, but more than Ms. Brody. Mr. Rhodes has more seniority than Ms. West, but less than Mr. Temple. Mr. Temple doesn't want the job. Who will be the new math department chairperson?

a. Mr. Rhodes
b. Mr. Temple
c. Ms. West
d. Ms. Brody

408. Four people witnessed a mugging. Each gave a different description of the mugger. Which description is probably right?

a. He was average height, thin, and middle-aged.
b. He was tall, thin, and middle-aged.
c. He was tall, thin, and young.
d. He was tall, of average weight, and middle-aged.

409. As they prepare for the state championships, one gymnast must be moved from the Level 2 team to the Level 1 team. The coaches will move the gymnast who has won the biggest prize and who has the most experience. In the last competition, Roberta won a bronze medal and has competed seven times before. Jamie has won a silver medal and has competed fewer times than Roberta. Beth has won a higher medal than Jamie and has competed more times than Roberta. Michele has won a bronze medal, and it is her third time competing. Who will be moved to the Level 1 team?

a. Roberta
b. Beth
c. Michele
d. Jamie

410. Four defensive football players are chasing the opposing wide receiver, who has the ball. Calvin is directly behind the ball carrier. Jenkins and Burton are side by side behind Calvin. Zeller is behind Jenkins and Burton. Calvin tries for the tackle but misses and falls. Burton trips. Which defensive player tackles the receiver?

a. Burton
b. Zeller
c. Jenkins
d. Calvin

411. Danielle has been visiting friends in Ridgewood for the past two weeks. She is leaving tomorrow morning and her flight is very early. Most of her friends live fairly close to the airport. Madison lives ten miles away. Frances lives five miles away, Samantha, seven miles. Alexis is farther away than Frances, but closer than Samantha. Approximately how far away from the airport is Alexis?

a. nine miles
b. seven miles
c. eight miles
d. six miles

412. Ms. Forest likes to let her students choose who their partners will be; however, no pair of students may work together more than seven class periods in a row. Adam and Baxter have studied together seven class periods in a row. Carter and Dennis have worked together three class periods in a row. Carter does not want to work with Adam. Who should be assigned to work with Baxter?

a. Carter
b. Adam
c. Dennis
d. Forest

413. At the baseball game, Henry was sitting in seat 253. Marla was sitting to the right of Henry in seat 254. In the seat to the left of Henry was George. Inez was sitting to the left of George. Which seat is Inez sitting in?

a. 251

b. 254

c. 255

d. 256

▶ **Set 28** (Answers begin on page 131.)

Questions that involve analytical reasoning—better known as "logic games"—tend to inspire fear in most test takers. These games give the most trouble to test takers who haven't defined a specific method for solving these problems. The best way to attack logic games is to have a plan. When solving the problems in this set, try the following strategy:

1. Know the rules of the logic game and what each rule means.
2. Draw up an easy-to-reference diagram that includes all of the game's information.
3. Look for common elements in the rules; you can combine these to make deductions.
4. Read the questions carefully; be sure you know what is being asked before you try to answer the question.

Now, try solving the logic games in this set.

Answer questions 414 through 416 on the basis of the information below.

The government of an island nation is in the process of deciding how to spend its limited income. It has $7 million left in its budget and eight programs to choose among. There is no provision in the constitution to have a surplus, and each program has requested the minimum amount they need; in other words, no program may be partially funded. The programs and their funding requests are:

- Hurricane preparedness: $2.5 million
- Harbor improvements: $1 million
- School music program: $0.5 million
- Senate office building remodeling: $1.5 million
- Agricultural subsidy program: $2 million
- National radio: $0.5 million
- Small business loan program: $3 million
- International airport: $4 million

414. If the legislature decides to fund the agricultural subsidy program, national radio, and the small business loan program, the only other single program that can be funded is
a. hurricane preparedness.
b. harbor improvements.
c. school music program.
d. senate office building remodeling.
e. international airport.

415. If the legislature decides to fund the agricultural subsidy program, national radio, and the small business loan program, what two other programs could they fund?
a. harbor improvements and international airport
b. harbor improvements and school music program
c. hurricane preparedness and school music program
d. hurricane preparedness and international airport
e. harbor improvements and hurricane preparedness

416. Senators from urban areas are very concerned about assuring that there will be funding for a new international airport. Senators from rural areas refuse to fund anything until money for agricultural subsidies is appropriated. If the legislature funds these two programs, on which of the following could they spend the rest of the money?
a. the school music program and national radio
b. hurricane preparedness
c. harbor improvements and the school music program
d. small business loan program
e. national radio and senate office building remodeling

Answer questions 417 through 418 on the basis of the information below.

A weekly television show routinely stars six actors, J, K, L, M, N, and O. Since the show has been on the air for a long time, some of the actors are good friends and some do not get along at all. In an effort to keep peace, the director sees to it that friends work together and enemies do not. Also, as the actors have become more popular, some of them need time off to do other projects. To keep the schedule working, the director has a few things she must be aware of:

- J will only work on episodes on which M is working.
- N will not work with K under any circumstances.
- M can only work every other week, in order to be free to film a movie
- At least three of the actors must appear in every weekly episode.

417. In a show about L getting a job at the same company J already works for and K used to work for, all three actors will appear. Which of the following is true about the other actors who may appear?
   a. M, N, and O must all appear.
   b. M may appear and N must appear.
   c. M must appear and O may appear.
   d. O may appear and N may appear.
   e. Only O may appear.

418. Next week, the show involves N's new car and O's new refrigerator. Which of the following is true about the other actors who may appear?
   a. M, J, L, and K all may appear.
   b. J, L, and K must appear.
   c. Only K may appear.
   d. Only L may appear.
   e. L and K must appear.

Answer questions 419 through 421 on the basis of the information below.

A cinema complex with six movie theaters never shows the same movie in more than one theater. None of the theaters is the same size as any other, with number 1 being the largest and going in order to number 6, the smallest. The theater also has the following rules:

- It will never show more than two R-rated movies at once.
- It will always show at least one G-rated movie and one PG-rated movie in the two middle-sized theaters (theaters 3 and 4).
- It will never show more than one foreign film at a time and never in the biggest theater.
- The starting times of movies will be staggered by fifteen minutes and will always be on the quarter hour.
- Employees need twenty minutes between showings to clean the theaters.

The cinema has the following films to choose from this particular week:

Shout, rated R
Que Pasa, a Spanish film rated PG
Abra Cadabra, rated G
Lessons, rated R
Jealousy, rated PG
Mist, a Swedish film rated R
Trek, rated NC-17
Fly, rated G

419. Which one of the following is an acceptable listing of films to show this week?
   a. *Shout, Mist, Trek, Que Pasa, Fly,* and *Jealousy*
   b. *Shout, Mist, Trek, Fly, Jealousy,* and *Abra Cadabra*
   c. *Que Pasa, Lessons, Mist, Shout, Abra Cadabra,* and *Trek*
   d. *Shout, Lessons, Mist, Trek, Fly,* and *Jealousy*
   e. *Shout, Fly, Trek, Lessons, Abra Cadabra,* and *Mist*

420. If *Shout* starts at 8:30, *Mist* at 8:15, *Trek* at 8:00, *Fly* at 7:45, *Jealousy* at 7:30, and *Abra Cadabra* at 7:15, and each movie is exactly two hours long, at what time will the next showing of *Trek* start?
   a. 10:00
   b. 10:15
   c. 10:30
   d. 10:45
   e. 11:00

421. The movies this week are showing in the following theaters:

Theater 1: *Shout*

Theater 2: *Trek*

Theater 3: *Abra Cadabra*

Theater 4: *Jealousy*

Theater 5: *Fly*

Theater 6: *Mist*

Shout is doing the most business, followed by *Trek* and, to the management's surprise, *Mist*. The management wants to move *Mist* to a larger theater. Which theater is the most logical?
   a. theater 1
   b. theater 2
   c. theater 3
   d. theater 4
   e. theater 5

Answer questions 422 through 423 on the basis of the information below.

The six top songs (not in order) of 1968 were:

"People Got to Be Free" by The Rascals
"Sittin' on the Dock of the Bay" by Otis Redding
"Honey" by Bobby Goldsboro
"Sunshine of Your Love" by Cream
"Love Is Blue" by Paul Mauriat & His Orchestra
"Hey Jude" by The Beatles

Here are some rules about the order of the songs:

- The Beatles and Cream do not appear next to each other on the list.
- The number 1 song is not "Love Is Blue."
- The songs by individual artists are numbers 3 and 4.
- The Rascals appear right before Cream and right after Otis Redding.

422. Which of the following is true?
   a. Song #3 is "Honey" by Bobby Goldsboro.
   b. Song #6 is "Hey Jude" by the Beatles.
   c. Song #1 is "Sittin' on the Dock of the Bay" by Otis Redding.
   d. Song #1 is "Sunshine of Your Love" by Cream.
   e. Song #3 is "Sittin' on the Dock of the Bay" by Otis Redding.

423. Which of the following is the correct order of songs?
   a. "Honey," "Love Is Blue," "People Got to Be Free," "Sunshine of Your Love," "Sittin' on the Dock of the Bay," "Hey Jude"
   b. "Love Is Blue," "Hey Jude," "Honey," "Sittin' on the Dock of the Bay," "People Got to Be Free," "Sunshine of Your Love"
   c. "Sunshine of Your Love," "People Got to Be Free," "Sittin' on the Dock of the Bay," "Honey," "Love Is Blue," "Hey Jude"
   d. "Hey Jude," "Love Is Blue," "Honey," "Sittin' on the Dock of the Bay," "People Got to Be Free," "Sunshine of Your Love"
   e. "Honey," "Sittin' on the Dock of the Bay," "Hey Jude," "Sunshine of Your Love," "People Got to Be Free," "Love Is Blue"

▶ Set 29 (Answers begin on page 132.)

If you're having trouble after the first set of logic games, there's a bonus for you—a complete explanation of questions 424 and 425 in the answers section, with a step-by-step explanation of how to set up a table to answer the questions.

Answer questions 424 and 425 on the basis of the information below.

At a Halloween party where people were asked to dress as an object that represented their professions, Quentin, Rachel, Sarah, Thomas, and Ulysses were among the guests. The costumes included a flower, a pencil, a spoon, a camera, and a thermometer. The professions included a photographer, a florist, a doctor, an accountant, and a chef.

- Quentin is an accountant.
- Neither Rachel nor Sarah was dressed as a spoon.
- None of the men is a doctor.
- Thomas is dressed as a camera.
- Sarah is a florist.

424. Which person is dressed as a thermometer?
  a. Quentin
  b. Rachel
  c. Sarah
  d. Thomas
  e. Ulysses

425. What is Ulysses's profession?
  a. photographer
  b. florist
  c. doctor
  d. accountant
  e. chef

Answer questions 426 through 428 on the basis of the information below.

Evan is a waiter in a café. After he turns in orders for the six people sitting at the counter—each of whom is eating alone and is sitting in chairs numbered 1 through 6—the cook opens a window in the kitchen and the order slips get messed up. Here's what Evan remembers about the orders:

- The entree orders are: fried eggs, a hamburger, a cheeseburger, a vegetable burger, soup, and a ham sandwich.
- The two people who did not order sandwiches are sitting at chairs 3 and 4.
- The person who ordered the cheeseburger and the one who ordered the hamburger are not sitting next to each other.
- The person in chair number 5 is a regular. She will not sit next to anyone who is eating ham.
- The person eating the vegetable burger is not sitting in chair 2, but is sitting between the person who ordered fried eggs and the one who ordered a cheeseburger.
- The customer who ordered the hamburger is not sitting next to the customer who ordered soup.

426. To which customer should Evan serve the vegetable burger?
  a. the customer in chair 2
  b. the customer in chair 3
  c. the customer in chair 4
  d. the customer in chair 5
  e. the customer in chair 6

427. To which customer should Evan serve the soup?
   a. the customer in chair 1
   b. the customer in chair 2
   c. the customer in chair 3
   d. the customer in chair 4
   e. the customer in chair 5

428. To which customer should Evan serve the ham sandwich?
   a. the customer in chair 1
   b. the customer in chair 2
   c. the customer in chair 4
   d. the customer in chair 5
   e. the customer in chair 6

Use the additional information below, along with the information before question 426, to answer questions 429 and 430.

Now Evan has to decide who gets which side dish. Here is what he remembers, in addition to the previous information, about the orders, which were: cole slaw, hash browns, onion rings, potato salad, french fries, and lettuce salad.

- The person who ordered soup did not order french fries, hash browns, onion rings, or a lettuce salad.
- The person who ordered onion rings is sitting in chair 6.
- The person who ordered potato salad is sitting between the person who ordered cole slaw and the one who ordered hash browns.
- The person who ordered a vegetable burger ordered a lettuce salad.
- The hash browns were ordered by the customer who ordered fried eggs.

429. With which entrée does the potato salad belong?
   a. soup
   b. hamburger
   c. cheeseburger
   d. fried eggs
   e. ham sandwich

430. With which entrée do the french fries belong?
   a. soup
   b. cheeseburger
   c. hamburger
   d. fried eggs
   e. ham sandwich

Answer questions 431 through 433 on the basis of the information below.

At a small company, parking spaces are reserved for the top executives: CEO, president, vice president, secretary, and treasurer—with the spaces lined up in that order. The parking lot guard can tell at a glance if the cars are parked correctly by looking at the color of the cars. The cars are yellow, green, purple, red, and blue, and the executives' names are Alice, Bert, Cheryl, David, and Enid.

- The car in the first space is red.
- A blue car is parked between the red car and the green car.
- The car in the last space is purple.
- The secretary drives a yellow car.
- Alice's car is parked next to David's.
- Enid drives a green car.
- Bert's car is parked between Cheryl's and Enid's.
- David's car is parked in the last space.

431. What color is the vice president's car?
    a. green
    b. yellow
    c. blue
    d. purple
    e. red

432. Who is the CEO?
    a. Alice
    b. Bert
    c. Cheryl
    d. David
    e. Enid

433. Who is the secretary?
    a. Enid
    b. David
    c. Cheryl
    d. Bert
    e. Alice

▶ **Set 30** (Answers begin on page 134.)

Remember, the best way to answer these logic game questions is to attack the information systematically. Make a diagram outlining all the given information. There's always at least one fact that can serve as your starting point, the place to begin eliminating possibilities.

Answer questions 434 through 436 on the basis of the information below.

Five towns—Fulton, Groton, Hudson, Ivy, and Jersey—which are covered by the same newspaper, all have excellent soccer teams. The teams are named the Panthers, the Whippets, the Antelopes, the Kangaroos, and the Gazelles. The sports reporter, who has just started at the newspaper, has to be careful not to get them confused. Here is what she knows:

- The team in Fulton has beaten the Antelopes, Panthers, and Kangaroos.
- The Whippets have beaten the teams in Jersey, Hudson, and Fulton.
- The Antelopes are in Groton.
- The team in Hudson is not the Kangaroos.

434. Where are the Whippets?
  a. Fulton
  b. Groton
  c. Hudson
  d. Ivy
  e. Jersey

435. Where are the Panthers?
  a. Ivy
  b. Jersey
  c. Fulton
  d. Groton
  e. Hudson

436. What team is in Fulton?
  a. Panthers
  b. Gazelles
  c. Whippets
  d. Kangaroos
  e. Antelopes

Answer questions 437 through 439 on the basis of the information below.

Henri delivers flowers for a local florist. One lovely day, he left the windows open on the delivery van and the cards all blew off the bouquets. He has to figure out who gets which flowers. He has five bouquets, each of which has only one kind of flower: daisies, roses, carnations, iris, and gladioli. He has five cards with names on them: a birthday card for Inez, a congratulations-on-your-promotion card for Jenny, a graduation card for Kevin, an anniversary card for Liz, and a housewarming card for Michael. Here's what Henri knows:

- Roses are Jenny's favorite flower and what her friends always send.
- Gladioli are traditionally sent for a housewarming.
- Kevin is allergic to daisies and iris.
- Liz is allergic to daisies and roses.
- Neither Liz nor Inez has moved recently.

437. Which flowers should be delivered to Kevin?
  a. carnations
  b. iris
  c. gladioli
  d. daisies
  e. roses

438. Who should get the housewarming gladioli?
  a. Jenny
  b. Kevin
  c. Liz
  d. Michael
  e. Inez

439. Which flowers should be delivered to Liz?
  a. gladioli
  b. daisies
  c. roses
  d. carnations
  e. iris

Answer questions 440 through 443 on the basis of the information below.

Five cities all got more rain than usual this year. The five cities are: Last Stand, Mile City, New Town, Olliopolis, and Polberg. The cities are located in five different areas of the country: the mountains, the forest, the coast, the desert, and in a valley. The rainfall amounts were: 12 inches, 27 inches, 32 inches, 44 inches, and 65 inches.

- The city in the desert got the least rain; the city in the forest got the most rain.
- New Town is in the mountains.
- Last Stand got more rain than Olliopolis.
- Mile City got more rain than Polberg, but less rain than New Town.
- Olliopolis got 44 inches of rain.
- The city in the mountains got 32 inches of rain; the city on the coast got 27 inches of rain.

440. Which city is in the desert?
  a. Last Stand
  b. Mile City
  c. New Town
  d. Olliopolis
  e. Polberg

441. Which city got the most rain?
  a. Last Stand
  b. Mile City
  c. New Town
  d. Olliopolis
  e. Polberg

442. How much rain did Mile City get?
  a. 12 inches
  b. 27 inches
  c. 32 inches
  d. 44 inches
  e. 65 inches

443. Where is Olliopolis located?
  a. the mountains
  b. the coast
  c. in a valley
  d. the desert
  e. the forest

▶ **Set 31** (Answers begin on page 135.)

Here's one more set of logic games. Remember, mapping out the game using all the given information is the most efficient way to attack this type of question.

Answer questions 444 through 447 on the basis of the information below.

Eleanor is in charge of seating the speakers at a table. In addition to the moderator, there will be a pilot, a writer, an attorney, and an explorer. The speakers' names are Gary, Heloise, Jarrod, Kate, and Lane.

- The moderator must sit in the middle, in seat #3.
- The attorney cannot sit next to the explorer.
- Lane is the pilot.
- The writer and the attorney sit on either side of the moderator.
- Heloise, who is not the moderator, sits between Kate and Jarrod.
- The moderator does not sit next to Jarrod or Lane.
- Gary, who is the attorney, sits in seat #4.

444. Who is the moderator?
   a. Lane
   b. Gary
   c. Heloise
   d. Kate
   e. Jarrod

445. Where does Jarrod sit?
   a. seat #1
   b. seat #2
   c. seat #3
   d. seat #4
   e. seat #5

446. What occupation does Jarrod hold?
   a. a moderator
   b. a pilot
   c. a writer
   d. an attorney
   e. an explorer

447. Who is the writer?
   a. Gary
   b. Heloise
   c. Jarrod
   d. Kate
   e. Lane

Answer question 448 on the basis of the information below.

Zinnia has a small container garden on her balcony. Each spring, she only has room to plant three vegetables. Because five vegetables are her favorites, she has worked out a schedule to plant each at least once every two years. The vegetables are: beans, cabbage, carrots, peppers, and tomatoes.

- Tomatoes are her favorites and she plants them every year.
- Each year, she plants only one vegetable that begins with the letter "C."
- She never plants carrots and peppers in the same year.
- She will plant cabbage in the second year.

448. In what order does she plant the vegetables in the next two years?
   a. first year: tomatoes, carrots, cabbage
      second year: tomatoes, peppers, beans
   b. first year: tomatoes, peppers, beans
      second year: cabbage, carrots, tomatoes
   c. first year: tomatoes, carrots, peppers
      second year: tomatoes, cabbage, beans
   d. first year: tomatoes, carrots, beans
      second year: tomatoes, cabbage, peppers
   e. first year: tomatoes, cabbage, peppers
      second year: carrots, cabbage, beans

Answer questions 449 through 453 on the basis of the information below.

Five roommates—Randy, Sally, Terry, Uma, and Vernon—each do one housekeeping task—mopping, sweeping, laundry, vacuuming, or dusting—one day a week, Monday through Friday.

- Vernon does not vacuum and does not do his task on Tuesday.
- Sally does the dusting, and does not do it on Monday or Friday.
- The mopping is done on Thursday.
- Terry does his task, which is not vacuuming, on Wednesday.
- The laundry is done on Friday, and not by Uma.
- Randy does his task on Monday.

449. When does Sally do the dusting?
   a. Friday
   b. Monday
   c. Tuesday
   d. Wednesday
   e. Thursday

450. What task does Terry do on Wednesday?
   a. vacuuming
   b. dusting
   c. mopping
   d. sweeping
   e. laundry

451. What day is the vacuuming done?
   a. Friday
   b. Monday
   c. Tuesday
   d. Wednesday
   e. Thursday

452. What task does Vernon do?
   a. vacuuming
   b. dusting
   c. mopping
   d. sweeping
   e. laundry

453. What day does Uma do her task?
   a. Monday
   b. Tuesday
   c. Wednesday
   d. Thursday
   e. Friday

▶ **Set 32** (Answers begin on page 136.)

Each of the questions in this set contains a short paragraph, and each paragraph presents an argument. Your task is to read the paragraph carefully and determine the main point the author is trying to make. What conclusion can be drawn from the argument? Each paragraph is followed by five statements. One statement supports the author's argument better than the others do. The best way to approach these questions is to first read the paragraph and then restate the author's main argument, or conclusion, in your own words.

454. If you're a fitness walker, there is no need for a commute to a health club. Your neighborhood can be your health club. You don't need a lot of fancy equipment to get a good workout either. All you need is a well-designed pair of athletic shoes.

This paragraph best supports the statement that
a. fitness walking is a better form of exercise than weight lifting.
b. a membership in a health club is a poor investment.
c. walking outdoors provides a better workout than walking indoors.
d. fitness walking is a convenient and valuable form of exercise.
e. poorly designed athletic shoes can cause major foot injuries.

455. It is well known that the world urgently needs adequate distribution of food, so that everyone gets enough. Adequate distribution of medicine is just as urgent. Medical expertise and medical supplies need to be redistributed throughout the world so that people in emerging nations will have proper medical care.

This paragraph best supports the statement that
a. the majority of the people in the world have never been seen by a doctor.
b. food production in emerging nations has slowed during the past several years.
c. most of the world's doctors are selfish about giving time and money to the poor.
d. the medical-supply industry should step up production of its products.
e. many people who live in emerging nations are not receiving proper medical care.

456. The criminal justice system needs to change. The system could be more just if it allowed victims the opportunity to confront the person who has harmed them. Also, mediation between victims and their offenders would give the offenders a chance to apologize for the harm they have done.

This paragraph best supports the statement that victims of a crime should
a. learn to forgive their offenders.
b. have the right to confront their offenders.
c. learn the art of mediation.
d. insist that their offenders be punished.
e. have the right to impose a sentence on their offenders.

457. In the past, consumers would rarely walk into an ice cream store and order low-fat ice cream. But that isn't the case today. An increasing health consciousness combined with a much bigger selection of tasty low-fat foods in all categories has made low-fat ice cream a very profitable item for ice cream store owners.

This paragraph best supports the statement that

a. low-fat ice cream produces more revenue than other low-fat foods.

b. ice cream store owners would be better off carrying only low-fat ice cream.

c. ice cream store owners no longer think that low-fat ice cream is an unpopular item.

d. low-fat ice cream is more popular than other kinds of ice cream.

e. consumers are fickle and it is impossible to please them.

458. A few states in this country are considering legislation that would prohibit schools from using calculators before the sixth grade. Other states take a different position. Some states are insisting on the purchase of graphing calculators for every student in middle school.

This paragraph best supports the statement that in this country

a. there are at least two opinions about the use of calculators in schools.

b. calculators are frequently a detriment to learning math.

c. state legislators are more involved in education than ever before.

d. the price of graphing calculators is less when schools buy in bulk.

e. the argument against calculators in schools is unfounded.

459. One of the warmest winters on record has put consumers in the mood to spend money. Spending is likely to be the strongest in thirteen years. During the month of February, sales of existing single-family homes hit an annual record rate of 4.75 million.

This paragraph best supports the statement that

a. consumer spending will be higher thirteen years from now than it is today.

b. more people buy houses in the month of February than in any other month.

c. during the winter months, the prices of single-family homes are the lowest.

d. there were about 4 million homes for sale during the month of February.

e. warm winter weather is likely to affect the rate of home sales.

460. One New York publisher has estimated that 50,000 to 60,000 people in the United States want an anthology that includes the complete works of William Shakespeare. And what accounts for this renewed interest in Shakespeare? As scholars point out, his psychological insights into both male and female characters are amazing even today.

This paragraph best supports the statement that

a. Shakespeare's characters are more interesting than fictional characters today.

b. people today are interested in Shakespeare's work because of the characters.

c. academic scholars are putting together an anthology of Shakespeare's work.

d. New Yorkers have a renewed interested in the work of Shakespeare.

e. Shakespeare was a psychiatrist as well as a playwright.

461. Today's workforce has a new set of social values. Ten years ago, a manager who was offered a promotion in a distant city would not have questioned the move. Today, a manager in that same situation might choose family happiness instead of career advancement.

This paragraph best supports the statement that

a. most managers are not loyal to the corporations for which they work.

b. businesses today do not understand their employees' needs.

c. employees' social values have changed over the past ten years.

d. career advancement is not important to today's business managers.

e. companies should require their employees to accept promotions.

462. Generation Xers are those people born roughly between 1965 and 1981. As employees, Generation Xers tend to be more challenged when they can carry out tasks independently. This makes Generation Xers the most entrepreneurial generation in history.

This paragraph best supports the statement that Generation Xers

a. work harder than people from other generations.

b. have a tendency to be self-directed workers.

c. have an interest in making history.

d. tend to work in jobs that require risk-taking behavior.

e. like to challenge their bosses' work attitudes.

463. Today's high school students spend too much time thinking about trivial and distracting matters such as fashion. Additionally, they often dress inappropriately on school grounds. Rather than spending time writing another detailed dress policy, we should make school uniforms mandatory. If students were required to wear uniforms, it would increase a sense of community and harmony in our schools and it would instill a sense of discipline in our students. Another positive effect would be that teachers and administrators would no longer have to act as clothing police, freeing them up to focus on more important issues.

This paragraph best supports the statement that

a. inappropriate clothing leads to failing grades.

b. students who wear school uniforms get into better colleges.

c. teachers and administrators spend at least 25% of their time enforcing the dress code.

d. students are not interested in being part of a community.

e. school uniforms should be compulsory for high school students.

▶ **Set 33** (Answers begin on page 138.)

For more practice with logical reasoning, try another set of questions that contain short paragraphs that make a specific argument. Remember, you are looking for the statement that is *best* supported by the information given in the passage.

464. Critical reading is a demanding process. To read critically, you must slow down your reading and, with pencil in hand, perform specific operations on the text. Mark up the text with your reactions, conclusions, and questions. When you read, become an active participant.

This paragraph best supports the statement that
a. critical reading is a slow, dull, but essential process.
b. the best critical reading happens at critical times in a person's life.
c. readers should get in the habit of questioning the truth of what they read.
d. critical reading requires thoughtful and careful attention.
e. critical reading should take place at the same time each day.

465. There are no effective boundaries when it comes to pollutants. Studies have shown that toxic insecticides that have been banned in many countries are riding the wind from countries where they remain legal. Compounds such as DDT and toxaphene have been found in remote places like the Yukon and other Arctic regions.

This paragraph best supports the statement that
a. toxic insecticides such as DDT have not been banned throughout the world.
b. more pollutants find their way into polar climates than they do into warmer areas.
c. studies have proven that many countries have ignored their own antipollution laws.
d. DDT and toxaphene are the two most toxic insecticides in the world.
e. even a worldwide ban on toxic insecticides would not stop the spread of DDT pollution.

466. The Fourth Amendment to the Constitution protects citizens against unreasonable searches and seizures. No search of a person's home or personal effects may be conducted without a written search warrant issued on probable cause. This means that a neutral judge must approve the factual basis justifying a search before it can be conducted.

This paragraph best supports the statement that the police cannot search a person's home or private papers unless they have
a. legal authorization.
b. direct evidence of a crime.
c. read the person his or her constitutional rights.
d. a reasonable belief that a crime has occurred.
e. requested that a judge be present.

467. During colonial times in America, juries were encouraged to ask questions of the parties in the courtroom. The jurors were, in fact, expected to investigate the facts of the case themselves. If jurors conducted an investigation today, we would throw out the case.

This paragraph best supports the statement that
a. juries are less important today than they were in colonial times.
b. jurors today are less interested in court cases than they were in colonial times.
c. courtrooms today are more efficient than they were in colonial times.
d. jurors in colonial times were more informed than jurors today.
e. the jury system in America has changed since colonial times.

468. Mathematics allows us to expand our consciousness. Mathematics tells us about economic trends, patterns of disease, and the growth of populations. Math is good at exposing the truth, but it can also perpetuate misunderstandings and untruths. Figures have the power to mislead people.

This paragraph best supports the statement that
a. the study of mathematics is dangerous.
b. words are more truthful than figures.
c. the study of mathematics is more important than other disciplines.
d. the power of numbers is that they cannot lie.
e. figures are sometimes used to deceive people.

469. Human technology developed from the first stone tools about two and a half million years ago. At the beginning, the rate of development was slow. Hundreds of thousands of years passed without much change. Today, new technologies are reported daily on television and in newspapers.

This paragraph best supports the statement that
a. stone tools were not really technology.
b. stone tools were in use for two and a half million years.
c. there is no way to know when stone tools first came into use.
d. In today's world, new technologies are constantly being developed.
e. none of the latest technologies is as significant as the development of stone tools.

470. Obesity is a serious problem in this country. Research suggests that obesity can lead to a number of health problems including diabetes, asthma, and heart disease. Recent research has even indicated that there may be a relationship between obesity and some types of cancer. Major public health campaigns that increase awareness and propose simple lifestyle changes that will, with diligence and desire, eliminate or least mitigate the incidence of obesity are a crucial first step in battling this critical problem.

This paragraph best supports the statement that

a. public health campaigns that raise consciousness and propose lifestyle changes are a productive way to fight obesity.

b. obesity is the leading cause of diabetes in our country.

c. people in our country watch too much television and do not exercise enough.

d. a decline in obesity would radically decrease the incidence of asthma.

e. fast-food restaurants and unhealthy school lunches contribute greatly to obesity.

471. In the 1966 Supreme Court decision *Miranda v. Arizona*, the court held that before the police can obtain statements from a person subjected to an interrogation, the person must be given a *Miranda* warning. This warning means that a person must be told that he or she has the right to remain silent during the police interrogation. Violation of this right means that any statement that the person makes is not admissible in a court hearing.

This paragraph best supports the statement that

a. police who do not warn persons of their *Miranda* rights are guilty of a crime.

b. a *Miranda* warning must be given before a police interrogation can begin.

c. the police may no longer interrogate persons suspected of a crime unless a lawyer is present.

d. the 1966 Supreme Court decision in *Miranda* should be reversed.

e. persons who are interrogated by police should always remain silent until their lawyer comes.

472. Walk into any supermarket or pharmacy and you will find several shelves of products designed to protect adults and children from the sun. Additionally, a host of public health campaigns have been created, including National Skin Cancer Awareness Month, that warn us about the sun's damaging UV rays and provide guidelines about protecting ourselves. While warnings about the sun's dangers are frequent, a recent survey found that fewer than half of all adults adequately protect themselves from the sun.

This paragraph best supports the statement that
a. children are better protected from the sun's dangerous rays than adults.
b. sales of sun protection products are at an all-time high.
c. adults are not heeding the warnings about the dangers of sun exposure seriously enough.
d. more adults have skin cancer now than ever before.
e. there is not enough information disseminated about the dangers of sun exposure.

473. Yoga has become a very popular type of exercise, but it may not be for everyone. Before you sign yourself up for a yoga class, you need to examine what it is you want from your fitness routine. If you're looking for a high-energy, fast-paced aerobic workout, a yoga class might not be your best choice.

This paragraph best supports the statement that
a. yoga is more popular than high-impact aerobics.
b. before embarking on a new exercise regimen, you should think about your needs and desires.
c. yoga is changing the world of fitness in major ways.
d. yoga benefits your body and mind.
e. most people think that yoga isn't a rigorous form of exercise.

▶ **Set 34** (Answers begin on page 140.)

Here's one more set of questions based on short paragraphs that make a specific argument. You will sometimes have to use inference—reading between the lines—to see which statement is *best* supported by the passage.

474. For too long, school cafeterias, in an effort to provide food they thought would be appetizing to young people, mimicked fast-food restaurants, serving items such as burgers and fries, pizza, hot dogs, and fried chicken. School districts nationwide are now addressing this trend by incorporating some simple and inexpensive options that will make cafeteria lunches healthier while still appealing to students.

This paragraph best supports the statement that
a. school cafeterias have always emphasized nutritional guidelines over any other considerations.
b. young people would rather eat in a school cafeteria than a local fast-food restaurant.
c. school lunch menus are becoming healthier due to major new initiatives on the part of school districts.
d. it is possible to make school lunches both healthier and appealing without spending a great deal of money and undertaking a radical transformation.
e. vegetarian lunch options would greatly improve the nutritional value of the school lunch program.

475. During the last six years, the number of practicing physicians has increased by about 20%. During the same time period, the number of healthcare managers has increased by more than 600%. These percentages mean that many doctors have lost the authority to make their own schedules, determine the fees that they charge, and decide on prescribed treatments.

This paragraph best supports the statement that doctors
a. resent the interference of healthcare managers.
b. no longer have adequate training.
c. care a great deal about their patients.
d. are less independent than they used to be.
e. are making a lot less money than they used to make.

476. By the time they reach adulthood, most people can perform many different activities involving motor skills. Motor skills involve such diverse tasks as riding a bicycle, threading a needle, and cooking a dinner. What all these activities have in common is their dependence on precision and timing of muscular movement.

This paragraph best supports the statement that
a. most adults have not refined their motor skills.
b. all adults know how to ride a bicycle.
c. refined motor skills are specifically limited to adults.
d. children perform fewer fine motor activities in a day than adults do.
e. threading a needle is a precise motor skill.

477. Close-up images of Mars by the *Mariner 9* probe indicated networks of valleys that looked like the stream beds on Earth. These images also implied that Mars once had an atmosphere that was thick enough to trap the sun's heat. If this were true, something happened to Mars billions of years ago that stripped away the planet's atmosphere.

This paragraph best supports the statement that
a. Mars now has little or no atmosphere.
b. Mars once had a thicker atmosphere than Earth does.
c. the *Mariner 9* probe took the first pictures of Mars.
d. Mars is closer to the sun than Earth is.
e. Mars is more mountainous than Earth is.

478. Forest fires feed on decades-long accumulations of debris and leap from the tops of young trees into the branches of mature trees. Fires that jump from treetop to treetop can be devastating. In old-growth forests, however, the shade of mature trees keeps thickets of small trees from sprouting, and the lower branches of mature trees are too high to catch the flames.

This paragraph best supports the statement that
a. forest fire damage is reduced in old-growth forests.
b. small trees should be cut down to prevent forest fires.
c. mature trees should be thinned out to prevent forest fires.
d. forest fires do the most damage in old-growth forests.
e. old-growth forests have a larger accumulation of forest debris.

479. Originating in the 1920s, the Pyramid scheme is one of the oldest con games going. Honest people are often pulled in, thinking the scheme is a legitimate investment enterprise. The first customer to "fall for" the Pyramid scheme will actually make big money and will therefore persuade friends and relatives to join also. The chain then continues with the con artist who originated the scheme pocketing, rather than investing, the money. Finally, the pyramid collapses, but by that time, the scam artist will usually have moved out of town, leaving no forwarding address.

This paragraph best supports the statement that
a. it is fairly easy to spot a Pyramid scheme in the making.
b. the first customer of a Pyramid scheme is the most gullible.
c. the people who set up Pyramid schemes are able to fool honest people.
d. the Pyramid scheme had its heyday in the 1920s, but it's making a comeback.
e. the Pyramid scheme got its name from its structure.

480. Most Reality TV centers on two common motivators: fame and money. The shows transform waitresses, hairdressers, investment bankers, counselors, and teachers, to name a few, from obscure figures to household names. A lucky few successfully parlay their fifteen minutes of fame into celebrity. The luckiest stars of Reality TV also reap huge financial rewards for acts including eating large insects, marrying someone they barely know, and revealing their innermost thoughts to millions of people.

This paragraph best supports the statement that
a. the stars of Reality TV are interested in being rich and famous.
b. Reality TV is the best thing that has happened to network television in a long time.
c. for Reality TV stars, fame will last only as long as their particular television show.
d. traditional dramas and sitcoms are being replaced by Reality TV programming at an alarming rate.
e. Reality TV shows represent a new wave of sensationalistic, low quality programming.

481. The image of a knitter as an older woman sitting in a comfortable, old-fashioned living room with a basket of yarn at her feet and a bun in her hair is one of the past. As knitting continues to become more popular and increasingly trendy, it is much more difficult to describe the average knitter. Knitters today might be 18, 28, 40, or 65. They might live in a big urban center and take classes in a knitting shop that doubles as a café or they may gather in suburban coffee shops to support one another in knitting and other aspects of life. They could be college roommates knitting in their dorm room or two senior citizens knitting in a church hall. Even men are getting in the act. It would be incredibly difficult to come up with an accurate profile of a contemporary knitter to replace that image of the old woman with the basket of yarn!

This paragraph best supports the statement that
a. people are returning to knitting in an attempt to reconnect with simpler times.
b. knitting is now more of a group activity, as opposed to an individual hobby.
c. creating an accurate profile of a particular type of person depends on the people in this group having traits and characteristics in common.
d. today's knitters are much less accomplished than knitters of the past.
e. young people are turning to knitting in record numbers.

▶ **Set 35** (Answers begin on page 141.)

A typical logical reasoning question presents an argument and asks you to analyze it. You may be asked to draw further conclusions from the argument, determine what strengthens or weakens the argument, find flaws in the argument, or justify the argument. Success with these types of questions depends on your being able to understand the structure of the argument. Remember that every argument has a point of view. Every argument draws a conclusion and is generally supported with evidence. Study each passage to determine how each sentence contributes to the argument the speaker is trying to make. Then make sure you understand the question that is being asked before you choose from the five answer options.

Answer questions 482 and 483 on the basis of the information below.

According to last week's newspaper, doctors in large cities make more money than doctors in small towns or rural areas. It does not seem fair that just because a doctor's office is in a fancy building or at a fancy address, he or she can charge the patients more. Of course, some medical schools cost more than others, but basically all doctors spend a lot of money and a long time in school. There's no proof that graduates of the more expensive schools practice in big cities and graduates of the less expensive schools practice in small towns. All doctors should charge the same. Whether a patient goes to a doctor in a big city or small town, the cost should be the same.

482. A person seeking to refute the argument might argue that
  a. all doctors charge too much money and should lower their fees.
  b. medical practices are more expensive to maintain in large cities than in small towns and rural areas.
  c. doctors who owe student loans should charge more than other doctors.
  d. medical care from small-town doctors is better than medical care from large-city doctors.
  e. certain medical specialists should charge more than others.

483. A major flaw in the argument is that the speaker assumes that
  a. all doctors are specialists.
  b. all patients carry health insurance.
  c. all doctors have huge student loans.
  d. all patients take too much time.
  e. all doctors see the same number of patients.

Answer questions 484 and 485 on the basis of the information below.

English ought to be the official language of the United States. There is no reason for the government to spend money printing documents in several different languages, just to cater to people who cannot speak English. The government has better ways to spend our money. People who come to this country should learn to speak English right away.

484. Which of the following, if true, would make the speaker's argument stronger?
  a. There is currently a law that says the government must provide people with documents in their native language.
  b. Most people in the United States who do not speak English were born here.
  c. Immigration rates have decreased in recent years.
  d. Many other countries have an official language.
  e. Canada has two official languages.

485. Which of the following, if true, would make the speaker's argument weaker?
  a. The government currently translates official documents into more than twenty languages.
  b. English is the most difficult language in the world to learn.
  c. Most people who immigrate to the United States learn English within two years of their arrival.
  d. Making English the official language is a politically unpopular idea.
  e. People who are bilingual are usually highly educated.

Answer questions 486 through 488 on the basis of the information below.

Some groups want to outlaw burning the flag. They say that people have fought and died for the flag and that citizens of the United States ought to respect that. But I say that respect cannot be legislated. Also, most citizens who have served in the military did not fight for the flag, they fought for what the flag represents. Among the things the flag represents is freedom of speech, which includes, I believe, the right for a citizen to express displeasure with the government by burning the flag in protest.

486. Which of the following best expresses the main point of the passage?
  a. Only veterans care about the flag-burning issue.
  b. Flag burning almost never happens, so outlawing it is a waste of time.
  c. Flag burning will be a very important issue in the next election.
  d. To outlaw flag burning is to outlaw what the flag represents.
  e. Burning the flag should only be illegal when it is done in foreign countries.

487. Which of the following, if true, would weaken the speaker's argument?
  a. An action is not considered a part of freedom of speech.
  b. People who burn the flag usually commit other crimes as well.
  c. The flag was not recognized by the government until 1812.
  d. State flags are almost never burned.
  e. Most people are against flag burning.

488. Which of the following is similar to the argument made by the speaker?
  a. The rich should not be allowed to "buy" politicians, so the Congress should enact campaign finance reform.
  b. The idea of freedom of religion also means the right not to participate in religion, so mandated school prayer violates freedom of religion.
  c. The Constitution guarantees freedom to own property, so taxes should be illegal.
  d. Convicted felons should not have their convictions overturned on a technicality.
  e. In order to understand what may be constitutional today, one needs to look at what the laws were when the Constitution was enacted.

▶ **Set 36** (Answers begin on page 142.)

Some logical reasoning questions ask you to determine the method the speaker is using when he or she presents the argument. Method-of-argument questions ask you to demonstrate an understanding of how a speaker's argument is put together. To determine the method of argument, again focus on the conclusion and on the evidence presented. What method does the speaker use to link the two?

Answer question 489 on the basis of the information below.

I know that our rules prohibit members from bringing more than one guest at a time to the club, but I think there should be an exception to the rule on Tuesdays, Wednesdays, and Thursdays. Members should be allowed to bring multiple guests on those days, since the majority of members use the club facilities on the other four days of the week.

489. The rules restricting the number of guests a member can bring to the club probably are intended to
   a. assure that members are not crowded by the presence of guests.
   b. provide extra income for the club on slow days.
   c. allow members to bring guests to the club for special events.
   d. restrict guests to public areas of the club.
   e. control the exact number of people in the club at any time.

Answer questions 490 and 491 on the basis of the information below.

A recent study on professional football players showed that this new ointment helps relieve joint pain. My mother has arthritis, and I told her she should try it, but she says it probably won't help her.

490. What argument should the mother use to point out why the ointment probably will not help her arthritis?
   a. The ointment was just experimental.
   b. The ointment is expensive.
   c. Football players' joint pain is not the result of arthritis.
   d. She has already tried another ointment and it didn't work.
   e. Football players are generally younger than she is.

491. Which of the following, if true, would strengthen the speaker's argument?
   a. The mother used to be a professional bowler.
   b. Football players' injuries are rarely painful.
   c. The mother's arthritis only flares up in bad weather.
   d. The mother finds exercise helps her arthritis.
   e. Football players who are injured tend to develop arthritis.

Answer questions 492 through 494 on the basis of the information below.

Giving children computers in grade school is a waste of money and teachers' time. These children are too young to learn how to use computers effectively and need to spend time on learning the basics, like arithmetic and reading. After all, a baby has to crawl before she can walk.

492. Which of the following methods of argument is used in the previous passage?
- **a.** a specific example that illustrates the speaker's point
- **b.** attacking the beliefs of those who disagree with the speaker
- **c.** relying on an analogy to prove the speaker's point
- **d.** displaying statistics that back up the speaker's point
- **e.** comparing different methods of learning

493. Which of the following, if true, would strengthen the speaker's argument?
- **a.** studies showing computers are expensive
- **b.** research on the effect of computer games on children
- **c.** examples of high school students who use computers improperly
- **d.** proof that the cost of computers is coming down
- **e.** evidence that using computers makes learning to read difficult

494. Which of the following, if true, would weaken the speaker's argument?
- **a.** a demonstration that computers can be used to teach reading and arithmetic
- **b.** analysis of the cost-effectiveness of new computers versus repairing old computers
- **c.** examples of adults who do not know how to use computers
- **d.** recent grade reports of students in the computer classes
- **e.** a visit to a classroom where computers are being used

Answer questions 495 and 496 on the basis of the information below.

The corner of Elm and Third needs to have a stoplight. Children cross this intersection on the way to school, and sometimes, they do not check for traffic. I've seen several children almost get hit by cars at this corner. I know that stoplights are not cheap, and I know that children cannot be protected from every danger, but this is one of the worst intersections in town. There needs to be a stoplight here so that traffic will be slowed down and the children can walk more safely.

495. Which of the following methods of argument is used in the above passage?
- **a.** analogy—comparing the intersection to something dangerous
- **b.** emotion—referring to the safety of children to get people interested
- **c.** statistical analysis—noting the number of children almost hit and the cost of a stop light
- **d.** personalization—telling the story of one child's near accident at the intersection
- **e.** attack—pointing out that people who are against the stoplight do not care about children

496. Which of the following, if true, would weaken the speaker's argument?
- **a.** Sometimes, cars run red lights.
- **b.** Fewer children are injured at corners that have stoplights.
- **c.** If parents teach their children basic traffic safety, then they might remember to look for cars.
- **d.** Children from this neighborhood used to take the bus to a school farther away.
- **e.** In the last year, there have only been three minor accidents at the intersection and none of them involved children.

▶ **Set 37** (Answers begin on page 143.)

Another type of logical reasoning question presents you with two different speakers talking about the same issue. Sometimes, the speakers' arguments overlap; in other words, they support each other. Sometimes, the speakers are presenting opposing viewpoints. For these items, make sure you understand the conclusion of *both* speakers before you attempt to answer the questions.

Answer questions 497 and 498 on the basis of the information below.

> **Frances:** Studies show that eating a healthy breakfast improves young children's ability to learn. However, it is not the responsibility of the schools to provide this meal; it is the responsibility of each child's parents.

> **Lars:** Although it would be nice if the schools could provide each child with a healthy breakfast, the cost of doing that takes money away from other, more important learning resources, such as the purchase of new computers. In the long run, children learn more when the schools concentrate on the services they traditionally provide and the parents do what they are supposed to do.

497. In what way does Lars's comment relate to Frances's?
   a. It weakens Frances's argument by changing the focus of the discussion.
   b. It strengthens Frances's argument by providing support for her premise.
   c. It states the logical outcome of Frances's views.
   d. It cannot be true if Frances's assertion about parental responsibility is true.
   e. It provides an argument that is the opposite of Frances's views.

498. What main assumption underlies each statement?
   a. As teachers become more scarce, schools will have to learn to be more cost-effective in recruiting new teachers.
   b. In the information age, the equipment schools must purchase for their students is getting more expensive.
   c. The study about students and breakfast is inconclusive at best, and more studies should be conducted to find out if school breakfasts are healthy.
   d. Schools have never had the responsibility for supplying students with breakfast; rather, they spend their money on teachers, books, and other tangibles of education.
   e. Parents are not assuming enough responsibility for their children's education and should become more involved in school issues.

Answer questions 499 through 501 on the basis of the information below.

Quinn: Our state is considering raising the age at which a person can get a driver's license to eighteen. This is unfair because the age has been sixteen for many years and sixteen-year-olds today are no less responsible than their parents and grandparents were at sixteen. Many young people today who are fourteen and fifteen years old are preparing to receive their licenses by driving with a learner's permit and a licensed driver, usually one of their parents. It would not be fair to suddenly say they have to wait two more years.

Dakota: It is true that people have been allowed to receive a driver's license at sixteen for generations. However, in recent years, the increase in traffic means drivers face more dangers than ever and must be ready to respond to a variety of situations. The fact that schools can no longer afford to teach drivers' education results in too many young drivers who are not prepared to face the traffic conditions of today.

499. What is the point at issue between Quinn and Dakota?
   a. whether sixteen-year-olds should be required to take drivers' education before being issued a license
   b. whether schools ought to provide drivers' education to fourteen- and fifteen-year-old students
   c. whether the standards for issuing drivers' licenses should become more stringent
   d. whether sixteen-year-olds are prepared to drive in today's traffic conditions
   e. whether parents are able to do a good job teaching their children to drive

500. On what does Quinn rely in making her argument?
   a. statistics
   b. emotion
   c. fairness
   d. anecdotes
   e. actualities

501. On what does Dakota rely in making her argument?
   a. statistics
   b. emotion
   c. fairness
   d. anecdotes
   e. actualities

Answers

▶ **Set 1** (Page 2)

1. b. This is a simple addition series. Each number increases by 2.

2. b. This is a simple subtraction series. Each number is 6 less than the previous number.

3. c. This is an alternation with repetition series in which each number repeats itself and then increases by 7.

4. a. This is a simple subtraction series. Each number is 35 less than the previous number.

5. d. In this addition series, 1 is added to the first number; 2 is added to the second number; 3 is added to the third number; and so forth.

6. d. This is a simple addition series with a random number, 8, interpolated as every other number. In the series, 6 is added to each number except 8, to arrive at the next number.

7. a. This is an alternating addition and subtraction series. In the first pattern, 10 is subtracted from each number to arrive at the next. In the second, 5 is added to each number to arrive at the next.

8. b. This is an alternating number subtraction series. First, 2 is subtracted, then 4, then 2, and so on.

9. c. In this simple alternating subtraction and addition series; 1 is subtracted, then 2 is added, and so on.

10. d. This alternating addition series begins with 3; then 1 is added to give 4; then 3 is added to give 7; then 1 is added, and so on.

11. a. This is a simple alternating subtraction series, which subtracts 2, then 5.

12. c. In this alternating repetition series, the random number 21 is interpolated every other number into an otherwise simple addition series that increases by 2, beginning with the number 9.

13. b. In this series, each number is repeated, then 13 issubtracted to arrive at the next number.

14. c. This is a simple multiplication series. Each number is 3 times more than the previous number.

15. a. This is a simple division series. Each number is divided by 5.

16. b. This is a simple alternating addition and subtraction series. In the first pattern, 3 is added; in the second, 2 is subtracted.

17. b. This is an alternating multiplication and subtracting series: First, multiply by 2 and then subtract 8.

18. c. In this simple addition series, each number increases by 0.8.

19. d. In this simple subtraction series, each number decreases by 0.4.

20. b. This is a simple division series; each number is one-half of the previous number.

▶ Set 2 (Page 4)

21. b. In this simple subtraction series, each number is 6 less than the previous number.

22. c. In this simple addition series, each number is 5 greater than the previous number.

23. e. This is a simple subtraction with repetition series. It begins with 20, which is repeated, then 3 is subtracted, resulting in 17, which is repeated, and so on.

24. d. This is a simple addition series with a random number, 18, interpolated as every third number. In the series, 4 is added to each number except 18, to arrive at the next number.

25. a. In this alternating repetition series, a random number, 33, is interpolated every third number into a simple addition series, in which each number increases by 2.

26. b. This is a simple addition series, which begins with 2 and adds 6.

27. a. This is an alternating subtraction series with the interpolation of a random number, 5, as every third number. In the subtraction series, 3 is subtracted, then 4, then 3, and so on.

28. e. This is a simple alternating addition and subtraction series. First, 3 is added, then 1 is subtracted, then 3 is added, 1 subtracted, and so on.

29. b. This is a simple subtraction series in which a random number, 85, is interpolated as every third number. In the subtraction series, 10 is subtracted from each number to arrive at the next.

30. c. Here, every other number follows a different pattern. In the first series, 6 is added to each number to arrive at the next. In the second series, 10 is added to each number to arrive at the next.

31. e. This is an alternating addition series, in which 10 is added, then 5, then 10, and so on.

32. a. This is a subtraction series with repetition. Each number repeats itself and then decreases by 9.

33. e. This is an alternating subtraction series with repetition. There are two different patterns here. In the first, a number repeats itself; then 3 is added to that number to arrive at the next number, which also repeats. This gives the series 17, 17, 20, 20, 23, and so on. Every third number follows a second pattern, in which 3 is subtracted from each number to arrive at the next: 34, 31, 28.

34. d. This is an alternating addition series with a random number, 4, interpolated as every third number. In the main series, 1 is added, then 2 is added, then 1, then 2, and so on.

35. e. This is an alternating repetition series, in which a random number, 61, is interpolated as every third number into an otherwise simple subtraction series. Starting with the second number, 57, each number (except 61) is 7 less than the previous number.

36. d. Here is a simple addition series, which begins with 9 and adds 7.

37. c. This is an alternating repetition series, with a random number, 22, interpolated as every third number into an otherwise simple addition series. In the addition series, 4 is added to each number to arrive at the next number.

38. d. This is an alternating addition and subtraction series. In the first pattern, 2 is added to each number to arrive at the next; in the alternate pattern, 6 is subtracted from each number to arrive at the next.

39. d. In this simple addition series, each number is 5 more than the previous number.

40. b. This is an alternating addition series, with a random number, 21, interpolated as every third number. The addition series alternates between adding 3 and adding 4. The number 21 appears after each number arrived at by adding 3.

▶ **Set 3** (Page 6)

41. e. This is a simple subtraction series, in which 3 is subtracted from each number to arrive at the next.

42. e. This simple addition series adds 4 to each number to arrive at the next.

43. d. This is a simple subtraction series, in which 4 is subtracted from each number to arrive at the next.

44. d. Here, there are two alternating patterns, one addition and one subtraction. The first starts with 2 and increases by 2; the second starts with 44 and decreases by 3.

45. a. In this simple subtraction series, the numbers decrease by 3.

46. b. In this simple addition with repetition series, each number in the series repeats itself, and then increases by 12 to arrive at the next number.

47. b. This is an alternating addition and subtraction series, in which the addition of 4 is alternated with the subtraction of 3.

48. e. Two patterns alternate here, with every third number following the alternate pattern. In the main series, beginning with 4, 3 is added to each number to arrive at the next. In the alternating series, beginning with 26, 6 is subtracted from each number to arrive at the next.

49. c. This is an alternating addition series that adds 5, then 2, then 5, and so on.

50. d. In this simple subtraction with repetition series, each number is repeated, then 3 is subtracted to give the next number, which is then repeated, and so on.

51. b. Here, there are two alternating patterns, with every other number following a different pattern. The first pattern begins with 13 and adds 2 to each number to arrive at the next; the alternating pattern begins with 29 and subtracts 3 each time.

52. c. Here, every third number follows a different pattern from the main series. In the main series, beginning with 16, 10 is added to each number to arrive at the next. In the alternating series, beginning with 56, 12 is added to each number to arrive at the next.

53. a. This is an alternating addition series with repetition, in which a random number, 66, is interpolated as every third number. The regular series adds 2, then 3, then 2, and so on, with 66 repeated after each "add 2" step.

54. c. This is an alternating addition series, with a random number, 35, interpolated as every third number. The pattern of addition is to add 2, add 5, add 2, and so on. The number 35 comes after each "add 2" step.

55. e. This is an alternating subtraction series, which subtracts 5, then 2, then 5, and so on.

56. c. This is an alternating subtraction series in which 2 is subtracted twice, then 3 is subtracted once, then 2 is subtracted twice, and so on.

57. a. This is a simple addition series with repetition. It adds 3 to each number to arrive at the next, which is repeated before 3 is added again.

58. c. Here, there are two alternating patterns. The first begins with 17 and adds 2; the second begins with 32 and subtracts 3.

59. a. Two patterns alternate here. The first pattern begins with 10 and adds 2 to each number to arrive at the next; the alternating pattern begins with 34 and subtracts 3 each time.

60. a. This is an alternating repetition series. The number 32 alternates with a series in which each number decreases by 2.

▶ Set 4 (Page 8)

61. b. This is a simple alternating addition and subtraction series. The first series begins with 8 and adds 3; the second begins with 43 and subtracts 2.

62. d. In this simple addition with repetition series, each number in the series repeats itself, and then increases by 12 to arrive at the next number.

63. b. This is a simple subtraction series in which a random number, 93, is interpolated as every third number. In the subtraction series, 10 is subtracted from each number to arrive at the next.

64. a. Two series alternate here, with every third number following a different pattern. In the main series, 3 is added to each number to arrive at the next. In the alternating series, 5 is subtracted from each number to arrive at the next.

65. d. This series alternates the addition of 4 with the subtraction of 3.

66. a. In this series, 5 is added to the previous number; the number 70 is inserted as every third number.

67. d. This is an alternating division and addition series: First, divide by 2, and then add 8.

68. c. This is a simple multiplication series. Each number is 2 times greater than the previous number.

69. b. This is a multiplication series; each number is 3 times the previous number.

70. a. In this series, the letters progress by 1; the numbers decrease by 3.

71. b. In this series, the letters progress by 2, and the numbers increase by 2.

72. c. The letters decrease by 1; the numbers are multiplied by 2.

73. d. This is a simple addition series; each number is 3 more than the previous number.

74. c. This is a simple subtraction series; each number is 4 less than the previous number.

75. b. This is an alternating addition and subtraction series. Roman numbers alternate with Arabic numbers. In the Roman numeral pattern, each number decreases by 1. In the Arabic numeral pattern, each number increases by 1.

▶ **Set 5** (Page 10)

76. a. This series consists of letters in a reverse alphabetical order.

77. b. This is an alternating series in alphabetical order. The middle letters follow the order ABCDE. The first and third letters are alphabetical beginning with J. The third letter is repeated as a first letter in each subsequent three-letter segment.

78. b. Because the letters are the same, concentrate on the number series, which is a simple 2, 3, 4, 5, 6 series, and follows each letter in order.

79. d. The second and forth letters in the series, L and A, are static. The first and third letters consist of an alphabetical order beginning with the letter E.

80. c. The first two letters, PQ, are static. The third letter is in alphabetical order, beginning with R. The number series is in descending order beginning with 5.

81. c. The first letters are in alphabetical order with a letter skipped in between each segment: C, E, G, I, K. The second and third letters are repeated; they are also in order with a skipped letter: M, O, Q, S, U.

82. a. In this series, the third letter is repeated as the first letter of the next segment. The middle letter, A, remains static. The third letters are in alphabetical order, beginning with R.

83. d. In this series, the letters remain the same: DEF. The subscript numbers follow this series: $1,1,1$; $1,1,2$; $1,2,2$; $2,2,2$; $2,2,3$.

84. c. There are two alphabetical series here. The first series is with the first letters only: STUVW. The second series involves the remaining letters: CD, EF, GH, IJ, KL.

85. a. The middle letters are static, so concentrate on the first and third letters. The series involves an alphabetical order with a reversal of the letters. The first letters are in alphabetical order: F, G, H, I, J. The second and fourth segments are reversals of the first and third segments. The missing segment begins with a new letter.

86. a. This series consists of a simple alphabetical order with the first two letters of all segments: B, C, D, E, F, G, H, I, J, K. The third letter of each segment is a repetition of the first letter.

87. d. There are three series to look for here. The first letters are alphabetical in reverse: Z, Y, X, W, V. The second letters are in alphabetical order, beginning with A. The number series is as follows: 5, 4, 6, 3, 7.

▶ **Set 6** (Page 11)

88. b. Look at each segment. In the first segment, the arrows are both pointing to the right. In the second segment, the first arrow is up and the second is down. The third segment repeats the first segment. In the fourth segment, the arrows are up and then down. Because this is an alternating series, the two arrows pointing right will be repeated, so option **b** is the only possible choice.

89. b. Notice that in each segment, the figures are all the same shape, but the one in the middle is larger than the two on either side. Also, notice that one of the figures is shaded and that this shading alternates first right and then left. To continue this pattern in the third segment, you will look for a square. Choice **b** is correct because this choice will put the large square between the two smaller squares, with the shading on the right.

90. c. This is an alternating series. In the first segment, the letter "E" faces right, then down, then right. In the second segment, the letters all face down. To follow this pattern, in the fourth segment, the letters must all face up.

91. c. In this series, the shaded part inside the circle gets larger and then smaller.

92. d. Look for opposites in this series of figures. The first and second segments are opposites of each other. The same is true for the third and fourth segments.

93. a. Look carefully at the number of dots in each domino. The first segment goes from five to three to one. The second segment goes from one to three to five. The third segment repeats the first segment.

94. c. All four segments use the same figures: two squares, one circle, and one triangle. In the first segment, the squares are on the outside of the circle and triangle. In the second segment, the squares are below the other two. In the third segment, the squares on are the

inside. In the fourth segment, the squares are above the triangle and circle.

95. a. Look at each segment. You will notice that in each, the figure on the right and the figure on the left are the same; the figure in between is different. To continue this pattern in the last segment, the diamond on the left will be repeated on the right. Choice **a** is the only possible answer.

96. b. Each arrow in this continuing series moves a few degrees in a clockwise direction. Think of these arrows as the big hand on a clock. The first arrow is at noon. The last arrow before the blank would be 12:40. Choice **b**, the correct answer, is at 12:45.

97. c. Study the pattern carefully. In the first segment, two letters face right and the next two face left. The first letter in the second segment repeats the last letter of the previous segment. The same is true for the third segment. But the forth segment changes again; it is the opposite of the first segment, so the last two letters must face right.

98. d. This sequence concerns the number of sides on each figure. In the first segment, the three figures have one side, and then two sides, and then three sides. In the second segment, the number of sides increases and then decreases. In the third segment, the number of sides continues to decrease.

99. a. In this series, the figures increase the amount of shading by one-fourth and, once a square is completely shaded, starts over with an unshaded square. In the second segment, you will notice that the figure goes from completely shaded to completely unshaded. This is why choice **a** is the correct choice.

100. d. This is an alternating series. The first and third segments are repeated. The second segment is simply upside down.

101. d. In each of the segments, the figures alternate between one-half and one-fourth shaded.

► **Set 7** (Page 13)

102. c. A leopard, cougar, and lion all belong to the cat family; an elephant does not.

103. b. The couch, table, and chair are pieces of furniture; the rug is not.

104. a. The yarn, twine, and cord are all used for tying. The tape is not used in the same way.

105. b. The guitar, violin, and cello are stringed instruments; the flute is a wind instrument.

106. c. Tulip, rose, and daisy are all types of flowers. A bud is not.

107. d. Tire, steering wheel, and engine are all parts of a car.

108. d. Parsley, basil, and dill are types of herbs. Mayonnaise is not an herb.

109. b. A branch, leaf, and root are all parts of a tree. The dirt underneath is not a part of the tree.

110. d. The first three choices are all synonyms.

111. a. An index, glossary, and chapter are all parts of a book. Choice **a** does not belong because the book is the whole, not a part.

112. c. The noun, preposition, and adverb are classes of words that make up a sentence. Punctuation belongs in a sentence, but punctuation is not a class of word.

113. d. The cornea, retina, and pupil are all parts of the eye.

114. d. Rye, sourdough, and pumpernickel are types of bread. A loaf is not a bread type.

115. b. An ounce measures weight; the other choices measure length.

116. a. Freeway, interstate, and expressway are all high-speed highways; a street is for low-speed traffic.

117. b. Dodge, duck, and avoid are all synonyms meaning evade. Flee means to run away from.

118. c. Heading, body, and closing are all parts of a letter; the letter is the whole, not a part.

▶ Set 8 (Page 15)

119. d. The core, seeds, and pulp are all parts of an apple. A slice would be a piece taken out of an apple.

120. b. Unique, rare, and exceptional are all synonyms. Beautiful has a different meaning.

121. c. Biology, chemistry, and zoology are all branches of science. Theology is the study of religion.

122. a. A circle, oval, and sphere are all circular shapes with no angles. A triangle is a different kind of shape with angles and three straight sides.

123. a. Flourish, prosper, and thrive are all synonyms; excite does not mean the same thing.

124. d. Evaluate, assess, and appraise are all synonyms; instruct does not mean the same thing.

125. a. The lobster, crab, and shrimp are all types of crustaceans; an eel is a fish.

126. c. The scythe, knife, and saw are all cutting tools. Pliers are tools, but they are not used for cutting.

127. b. Two, six, and eight are all even numbers; three is an odd number.

128. c. A peninsula, island, and cape are all landforms; a bay is a body of water.

129. c. Seat, rung, and leg are all parts of a chair. Not all chairs have cushions.

130. d. Fair, just, and equitable are all synonyms meaning impartial. Favorable means expressing approval.

131. c. Defendant, prosecutor, and judge are all persons involved in a trial. A trial is not a person.

132. b. Area, circumference, and quadrilateral are all terms used in the study of geometry. Variable is a term generally used in the study of algebra.

133. b. The mayor, governor, and senator are all persons elected to government offices; the lawyer is not an elected official.

134. d. Acute, right, and obtuse are geometric terms describing particular angles. Parallel refers to two lines that never intersect.

135. c. The wing, fin, and rudder are all parts of an airplane.

136. a. The heart, liver, and stomach are all organs of the body. The aorta is an artery, not an organ.

▶ **Set 9** (Page 17)

137. b. The necessary part of a book is its pages; there is no book without pages. Not all books are fiction (choice **a**), and not all books have pictures (choice **c**). Learning (choice **d**) may or may not take place with a book.

138. d. A guitar does not exist without strings, so strings are an essential part of a guitar. A band is not necessary to a guitar (choice **a**). Guitar playing can be learned without a teacher (choice **b**). Songs are byproducts of a guitar (choice **c**).

139. a. All shoes have a sole of some sort. Not all shoes are made of leather (choice **b**); nor do they all have laces (choice **c**). Walking (choice **d**) is not essential to a shoe.

140. c. A person or animal must take in oxygen for respiration to occur. A mouth (choice **a**) is not essential because breathing can occur through the nose. Choices **b** and **d** are clearly not essential and can be ruled out.

141. b. An election does not exist without voters. The election of a president (choice **a**) is a byproduct. Not all elections are held in November (choice **c**), nor are they nationwide (choice **d**).

142. d. A diploma is awarded at graduation, so graduation is essential to obtaining a diploma. Employment may be a byproduct (choice **c**). A principal and a curriculum (choices **a** and **b**) may play a role in the awarding of some diplomas, but they are not essential.

143. c. Water is essential for swimming—without water, there is no swimming. The other choices are things that may or may not be present.

144. a. Without students, a school cannot exist; therefore, students are the essential part of schools. The other choices may be related, but they are not essential.

145. d. Words are a necessary part of language. Slang is not necessary to language (choice **b**). Not all languages are written (choice **c**). Words do not have to be spoken in order to be part of a language (choice **a**).

146. b. A desert is an arid tract of land. Not all deserts are flat (choice **d**). Not all deserts have cacti or oases (choices **a** and **c**).

147. a. Lightning is produced from a discharge of electricity, so electricity is essential. Thunder and rain are not essential to the production of lightning (choices **b** and **d**). Brightness may be a byproduct of lightning, but it is not essential (choice **c**).

148. b. The essential part of a monopoly is that it involves exclusive ownership or control.

149. d. To harvest something, one must have a crop, which is the essential element for this item. Autumn (choice **a**) is not the only time crops are harvested. There may not be enough of a crop to stockpile (choice **b**), and you can harvest crops without a tractor (choice **c**).

150. a. A gala indicates a celebration, the necessary element here. A tuxedo (choice **b**) is not required garb at a gala, nor is an appetizer (choice **c**). A gala may be held without the benefit of anyone speaking (choice **d**).

151. d. Pain is suffering or hurt, so choice **d** is the essential element. Without hurt, there is no pain. A cut (choice **a**) or a burn (choice **b**) may cause pain, but so do many other types of injury. A nuisance (choice **c**) is an annoyance that may or may not cause pain.

▶ **Set 10** (Page 19)

152. c. An infirmary is a place that takes care of the infirm, sick, or injured. Without patients, there is no infirmary. Surgery (choice **a**) may not be required for patients. A disease (choice **b**) is not necessary because the infirmary may only see patients with injuries. A receptionist (choice **d**) would be helpful but not essential.

153. b. A facsimile must involve an image of some sort. The image or facsimile need not, however, be a picture (choice **a**). A mimeograph and a copier machine (choices **c** and **d**) are just a two of the ways that images may be produced, so they do not qualify as the essential element for this item.

154. b. A domicile is a legal residence, so dwelling is the essential component for this item. You do not need a tenant (choice **a**) in the domicile, nor do you need a kitchen (choice **c**). A house (choice **d**) is just one form of a domicile (which could also be a tent, hogan, van, camper, motor home, apartment, dormitory, etc.).

155. d. A culture is the behavior pattern of a particular population, so customs are the essential element. A culture may or may not be civil or educated (choices **a** and **b**). A culture may be an agricultural society (choice **c**), but this is not the essential element.

156. a. A bonus is something given or paid beyond what is usual or expected, so reward is the essential element. A bonus may not involve a raise in pay or cash (choices **b** and **c**), and it may be received from someone other than an employer (choice **d**).

157. c. An antique is something that belongs to, or was made in, an earlier period. It may or may not be a rarity (choice **a**), and it does not have to be an artifact, an object produced or shaped by human craft (choice **b**). An antique is old but does not have to be prehistoric (choice **d**).

158. b. An itinerary is a proposed route of a journey. A map (choice **a**) is not necessary to have a planned route. Travel (choice **c**) is *usually* the outcome of an itinerary, but not always. A guidebook (choice **d**) may be used to plan the journey but is not essential.

159. c. An orchestra is a large group of musicians, so musicians are essential. Although many orchestras have violin sections, violins aren't essential to an orchestra (choice **a**). Neither a stage (choice **b**) nor a soloist (choice **d**) is necessary.

160. d. Knowledge is understanding gained through experience or study, so learning is the essential element. A school (choice **a**) is not necessary for learning or knowledge to take place, nor is a teacher or a textbook (choices **b** and **c**).

161. d. A dimension is a measure of spatial content. A compass (choice **a**) and ruler (choice **b**) may help determine the dimension, but other instruments may also be used, so these are not the essential element here. An inch (choice **c**) is only one way to determine a dimension.

162. a. Sustenance is something, especially food, that sustains life or health, so nourishment is the essential element. Water and grains (choices **b** and **c**) are components of nourishment, but other things can be taken in as well. A menu (choice **d**) may present a list of foods, but it is not essential to sustenance.

163. c. An ovation is prolonged, enthusiastic applause, so applause is necessary to an ovation. An outburst (choice **a**) may take place during an ovation; "bravo" (choice **b**) may or may not be uttered; and an encore (choice **d**) would take place *after* an ovation.

164. a. All vertebrates have a backbone. Reptiles (choice **b**) are vertebrates, but so are many other animals. Mammals (choice **c**) are vertebrates, but so are birds and reptiles. All vertebrates (choice **d**) are animals, but not all animals are vertebrates.

165.b. Provisions imply the general supplies needed, so choice **b** is the essential element. The other choices are byproducts, but they are not essential.

166.d. A purchase is an acquisition of something. A purchase may be made by trade (choice **a**) or with money (choice **b**), so those are not essential elements. A bank (choice **c**) may or may not be involved in a purchase.

▶ Set 11 (Page 21)

167. a. A dome is a large rounded roof or ceiling, so being rounded is essential to a dome. A geodesic dome (choice **b**) is only one type of dome. Some, but not all domes, have copper roofs (choice **d**). Domes are often found on government buildings (choice **c**), but domes exist in many other places.

168. b. A recipe is a list of directions to make something. Recipes may be used to prepare desserts (choice **a**), among other things. One does not need a cookbook (choice **c**) to have a recipe, and utensils (choice **d**) may or may not be used to make a recipe.

169. d. A hurricane cannot exist without wind. A beach is not essential to a hurricane (choice **a**). A hurricane is a type of cyclone, which rules out choice **b**. Not all hurricanes cause damage (choice **c**).

170. c. Without a signature, there is no autograph. Athletes and actors (choices **a** and **b**) may sign autographs, but they are not essential. An autograph can be signed with something other than a pen (choice **d**).

171. a. Residents must be present in order to have a town. A town may be too small to have skyscrapers (choice **b**). A town may or may not have parks (choice **c**) and libraries (choice **d**), so they are not the essential elements.

172. d. A wedding results in a joining, or a marriage, so choice **d** is the essential element. Love (choice **a**) usually precedes a wedding, but it is not essential. A wedding may take place anywhere, so a church (choice **b**) is not required. A ring (choice **c**) is often used in a wedding, but it is not necessary.

173. c. A faculty consists of a group of teachers and cannot exist without them. The faculty may work in buildings (choice **a**), but the buildings aren't essential. They may use textbooks (choice **b**) and attend meetings (choice **d**), but these aren't essential either.

174. a. A cage is meant to keep something surrounded, so enclosure is the essential element. A prisoner (choice **b**) or an animal (choice **c**) are two things that may be kept in cages, among many other things. A zoo (choice **d**) is only one place that has cages.

175. b. A directory is a listing of names or things, so choice **b** is the essential element. A telephone (choice **a**) often has a directory associated with it, but it is not essential. A computer (choice **c**) uses a directory format to list files, but it is not required. Names (choice **d**) are often listed in a directory, but many other things are listed in directories, so this is not the essential element.

176. a. An agreement is necessary to have a contract. A contract may appear on a document (choice **b**), but it is not required. A contract may be oral as well as written, so choice **c** is not essential. A contract can be made without an attorney (choice **d**).

177. b. A saddle is something one uses to sit on an animal, so it must have a seat (choice **b**). A saddle is often used on a horse (choice **a**), but it may be used on other animals. Stirrups (choice **c**) are often found on a saddle but may not be used. A horn (choice **d**) is found on Western saddles, but not English saddles, so it is not the essential element here.

178. a. Something cannot vibrate without creating motion, so motion is essential to vibration.

179. b. The essential part of a cell is its nucleus. Not all cells produce chlorophyll (choice **a**). Not all cells are nerve cells (choice **c**). All living things, not just humans (choice **d**), have cells.

180. c. Without a first-place win, there is no champion, so winning is essential. There may be champions in running, swimming, or speaking, but there are also champions in many other areas.

181.d. A glacier is a large mass of ice and cannot exist without it. A glacier can move down a mountain, but it can also move across a valley or a plain, which rules out choice **a**. Glaciers exist in all seasons, which rules out choice **b**. There are many glaciers in the world today, which rules out choice **c**.

► **Set 12** (Page 23)

182.b. Coffee goes into a cup and soup goes into a bowl. Choices **a** and **c** are incorrect because they are other utensils. The answer is not choice **d** because the word *food* is too general.

183.d. A gym is a place where people exercise. A restaurant is a place where people eat. Food (choice **a**) is not the answer because it is something people eat, not a place or location where they eat. The answer is not choice **b** or **c** because neither represents a place where people eat.

184. c. An oar puts a rowboat into motion. A foot puts a skateboard into motion. The answer is not choice **a** because running is not an object that is put into motion by a foot. Sneaker (choice **b**) is incorrect because it is something worn on a foot. Jumping (choice **d**) is incorrect because although you do need feet to jump, jumping is not an object that is put into motion by means of a foot.

185.d. A window is made up of panes, and a book is made up of pages. The answer is not choice **a** because a novel is a type of book. The answer is not choice **b** because glass has no relationship to a book. Choice **c** is incorrect because a cover is only one part of a book; a book is not made up of covers.

186. c. Secretly is the opposite of openly, and silently is the opposite of noisily. Choices **a** and **b** are clearly not the opposites of silently. Choice d means the same thing as silently.

187.b. An artist makes paintings; a senator makes laws. The answer is not choice **a** because an attorney does not make laws and a senator is not an attorney. Choice **c** is incorrect because a senator is a politician. Constituents (choice **d**) is also incorrect because a senator serves his or her constituents.

188.b. An actor performs in a play. A musician performs at a concert. Choices **a**, **c**, and **d** are incorrect because none is people who perform.

189. a. Careful and cautious are synonyms (they mean the same thing). Boastful and arrogant are also synonyms. The answer is not choice **b** because humble means the opposite of boastful. The answer is not choice **c** or **d** because neither means the same as boastful.

190.d. A group of lions is called a pride. A group of fish swim in a school. Teacher (choice **a**) and student (choice **b**) refer to another meaning of the word *school*. The answer is not choice **c** because self-respect has no obvious relationship to this particular meaning of school.

191. a. Guide and direct are synonyms, and reduce and decrease are synonyms. The answer is not choice **b** or **d** because neither means the same as reduce. Choice **c** is incorrect because increase is the opposite of reduce.

192.b. A yard is a larger measure than an inch (a yard contains 36 inches). A quart is a larger measure than an ounce (a quart contains 32 ounces). Gallon (choice **a**) is incorrect because it is larger than a quart. Choices **c** and **d** are incorrect because they are not units of measurement.

193. c. A lizard is a type of reptile; a daisy is a type of flower. Choices **a** and **b** are incorrect because a petal and a stem are parts of a flower, not types of flowers. Choice **d** is incorrect because an alligator is another type of reptile, not a type of flower.

194.b. Elated is the opposite of despondent; enlightened is the opposite of ignorant.

195.d. A marathon is a long race and hibernation is a lengthy period of sleep. The answer is not choice **a** or **b** because even though a bear and winter are related to hibernation, neither completes the analogy. Choice **c** is incorrect because sleep and dream are not synonymous.

196. a. If someone has been humiliated, they have been greatly embarrassed. If someone is terrified, they are extremely frightened. The answer is not choice **b** because an agitated person is not necessarily frightened. Choices **c** and **d** are incorrect because neither word expresses a state of being frightened.

197. d. An odometer is an instrument used to measure mileage. A compass is an instrument used to determine direction. Choices **a**, **b**, and **c** are incorrect because none is an instrument.

198. a. An optimist is a person whose outlook is cheerful. A pessimist is a person whose outlook is gloomy. The answer is not choice **b** because a pessimist does not have to be mean. Choices **c** and **d** are incorrect because neither adjective describes the outlook of a pessimist.

199. c. A sponge is a porous material. Rubber is an elastic material. Choice **a** is incorrect because rubber would not generally be referred to as massive. The answer is not choice **b** because even though rubber is a solid, its most noticeable characteristic is its elasticity. Choice **d** is incorrect because rubber has flexibility.

200. d. Candid and indirect refer to opposing traits. Honest and untruthful refer to opposing traits. The answer is not choice **a** because frank means the same thing as candid. Wicked (choice **b**) is incorrect because even though it refers to a negative trait, it does not mean the opposite of honest. Choice **c** is incorrect because truthful and honest mean the same thing.

201. d. A pen is a tool used by a poet. A needle is a tool used by a tailor. The answer is not choice **a**, **b**, or **c** because none is a person and therefore cannot complete the analogy.

▶ **Set 13** (Page 25)

202. d. A can of paint is to a paintbrush as a spool of thread is to a sewing needle. This is a relationship of function. Both show the tool needed to perform a task.

203. a. Grapes are to a pear as cheese is to butter. This relationship shows the grouping or category to which something belongs. Grapes and pears are fruit; cheese and butter are both dairy products.

204. d. An oar is to a canoe as a steering wheel is to a car. This is a functional relationship. The oar helps steer the canoe in the way that the steering wheel steers the car.

205. a. Cup is to bowl as vacuum cleaner is to broom. This is another relationship about function. The cup and bowl are both used for eating. The vacuum cleaner and broom are both used for cleaning.

206. d. Sheep are to sweater as pine trees are to log cabin. Wool comes from the sheep to make a sweater; wood comes from the trees to make the log cabin.

207. a. Hand is to ring as head is to cap. A ring is worn on a person's hand; a cap is worn on a person's head.

208. b. A palm tree is to a pine tree as a bathing suit is to a parka. This relationship shows an opposite—warm to cold. Palm trees grow in warm climates and pine trees grow in cold climates. Bathing suits are worn in warm weather; parkas are worn in cold weather.

209. d. Batteries are to a flashlight as telephone wires are to a telephone. The batteries provide power to the flashlight; the wires send power to the telephone.

210. d. A fish is to a dragonfly as a chicken is to corn. Fish eat insects; chickens eat corn.

211. a. A telephone is to a stamped letter as an airplane is to a bus. A telephone and letter are both forms of communication. An airplane and bus are both forms of transportation.

212. c. A trapeze performer is to a clown as swings are to a sliding board. This relationship shows a classification. Trapeze performers and clowns are found at circuses; swings and sliding boards are found on playgrounds.

213. c. Camera is to photograph as teakettle is to a cup of tea. The camera is used to make the photo; the teakettle is used to make the tea.

214. b. Hat and mittens are to desert as snorkel and flippers are to snow. This relationship shows an opposition. The hat and mittens are NOT worn in the desert; the snorkel and flippers are NOT worn in the snow.

215. d. Car is to horse and buggy as computer is to pen and ink. This relationship shows the difference between modern times and times past.

216. c. Leather boots are to cow as pearl necklace is to oyster. The leather to make the boots comes from a cow; the pearls to make the necklace come from oysters.

217. b. A toddler is to an adult as a caterpillar is to a butterfly. This relationship shows the young and the adult. The caterpillar is an early stage of the adult butterfly.

218. b. Towel is to bathtub as chest of drawers is to bed. The towel and bathtub are both found in a bathroom; the chest and the bed are both found in a bedroom.

219. a. A snow-capped mountain is to a crocodile as a cactus is to a starfish. This relationship shows an opposition. The crocodile does NOT belong on the mountain; the starfish does NOT belong in the desert.

220. c. A shirt is to a button as a belt is to a belt buckle. A button is used to close a shirt; a belt buckle is used to close a belt.

221. c. A penny is to a dollar as a small house is to a skyscraper. This relationship shows smaller to larger. A penny is much smaller than a dollar; a house is much smaller than a skyscraper.

▶ Set 14 (Page 31)

222. b. Guitar is to horn as hammer is to saw. This relationship is about grouping. The guitar and horn are musical instruments. The hammer and saw are carpentry tools.

223. d. Tree is to leaf as bird is to feather. This relationship shows part to whole. The leaf is a part of the tree; the feather is a part of the bird.

224. c. House is to tent as truck is to wagon. The house is a more sophisticated form of shelter than the tent; the truck is a more sophisticated mode of transportation than the wagon.

225. c. Scissors is to knife as pitcher is to watering can. This relationship is about function. The scissors and knife are both used for cutting. The pitcher and watering can are both used for watering.

226. b. A T-shirt is to a pair of shoes as a chest of drawers is to a couch. The relationship shows to which group something belongs. The T-shirt and shoes are both articles of clothing; the chest and couch are both pieces of furniture.

227. d. A bookshelf is to a book as a refrigerator is to a carton of milk. The book is placed on a bookshelf; the milk is placed in a refrigerator.

228. d. A squirrel is to an acorn as a bird is to a worm. A squirrel eats acorns; a bird eats worms.

229. b. An eye is to a pair of binoculars as a mouth is to a microphone. This relationship shows magnification. The binoculars help one see farther. The microphone helps one speak louder.

230. a. Knitting needles are to sweater as a computer is to a report. This relationship shows the tool needed to make a product. The knitting needles are used to create the sweater; the computer is used to write a report.

231. b. Bread is to knife as log is to ax. This relationship shows function. The knife cuts the bread; the ax chops the log.

232. b. Closet is to shirt as kitchen cabinets are to cans of food. The shirt is stored in the closet; the food is stored in the cabinets.

233. a. Pyramid is to triangle as cube is to square. This relationship shows dimension. The triangle shows one dimension of the pyramid; the square is one dimension of the cube.

234. c. Toothbrush is to toothpaste as butter knife is to butter. This relationship shows function. The toothbrush is used to apply the toothpaste to teeth; the knife is used to apply butter to bread.

235. c. Fly is to ant as snake is to lizard. The fly and ant are both insects; the snake and lizard are both reptiles.

236. a. Sail is to sailboat as pedal is to bicycle. The sail makes the sailboat move; the pedal makes the bicycle move.

237. d. Hose is to firefighter as needle is to nurse. This relationship shows the tools of the trade. A hose is a tool used by a firefighter; a needle is a tool used by a nurse.

238. c. A U.S. flag is to a fireworks display as a Halloween mask is to a pumpkin. This relationship shows symbols. The flag and fireworks are symbols of the Fourth of July. The mask and pumpkin are symbols of Halloween.

239. d. Newspaper is to book as trumpet is to banjo. The newspaper and book are to read; the trumpet and banjo are musical instruments to play.

240. b. Dishes are to kitchen sink as car is to hose. Dishes are cleaned in the sink; the car is cleaned with the hose.

241. a. The United States is to the world as a brick is to a brick house. This relationship shows part to whole. The United States is one part of the world; the brick is one part of the house.

▶ **Set 15** (Page 37)

242.b. The three above the line are all insects. The hamster and squirrel are rodents, so the correct choice is **b** because the mouse is also a rodent. The other three choices are not rodents.

243. a. In the relationship above the line, the saw and the nails are tools a carpenter uses. In the relationship below the line, the stethoscope and thermometer are tools a pediatrician uses.

244. c. A table made of wood could come from an oak tree. A shirt made of cloth could come from a cotton plant. Choice **a** looks like a reasonable answer if you apply the same sentence: "A shirt made of cloth could come from sewing." But this is not the same relationship as the one above the line. The oak and the cotton are both materials used to make the table and the shirt.

245.d. The words above the line show a continuum: Command is more extreme than rule, and dictate is more extreme than command. Below the line, the continuum is as follows: Sleep is more than doze, and hibernate is more than sleep. The other choices are not related in the same way.

246. a. A banquet and a feast are both large meals; a palace and a mansion are both large places of shelter.

247.b. A fence and a wall mark a boundary. A path and an alley mark a passageway.

248. c. The objects above the line are all things used by an artist. The objects below the line are all things used by a teacher.

249.b. The relationship above the line is that snow on a mountain creates conditions for skiing. Below the line, the relationship is that warmth at a lake creates conditions for swimming.

250.d. Above the line, the relationship shows a progression of sources of light. The relationship below the line shows a progression of types of housing, from smallest to largest. Choice **a** is incorrect because a tent is smaller than a house. Choices **b** and **c** are wrong because they are not part of the progression.

251. a. The relationship above the line is as follows; apples are a kind of fruit; fruit is sold in a supermarket. Below the line, the relationship is: a novel is a kind of book; books are sold in a bookstore.

252.d. The tadpole is a young frog; frogs are amphibians. The lamb is a young sheep; sheep are mammals. Animal (choice **a**) is incorrect because it is too large a grouping: Animals include insects, birds, mammals, reptiles, and amphibians. Choices **b** and **c** are incorrect because they are not part of the progression.

253.b. Walk, skip, and run represent a continuum of movement: Skipping is faster than walking; running is faster than skipping. Below the line, the continuum is about throwing: Pitch is faster than toss; hurl is faster than pitch.

254. c. The honeybee, angel, and bat all have wings; they are capable of flying. The kangaroo, rabbit, and grasshopper are all capable of hopping.

255. a. Above the line, the relationship is as follows: A daisy is a type of flower, and a flower is a type of plant. Below the line, the relationship is as follows: A bungalow is a type of house, and a house is a type of building.

► **Set 16** (Page 39)

256. b. A petal is a part of a flower; a tire is a part of a bicycle.

257. d. A bristle is a part of a brush; a key is a part of a piano.

258. a. A group of fish is a school; a group of wolves is a pack.

259. a. An odometer measures distance; a scale measures weight.

260. d. Siamese is a kind of cat; romaine is a kind of lettuce.

261. e. A pedal propels a bicycle; an oar propels a canoe.

262. c. Pulsate and throb are synonyms, as are examine and scrutinize.

263. c. An elephant is a pachyderm; a kangaroo is a marsupial.

264. e. Depressed is an intensification of sad; exhausted is an intensification of tired.

265. a. A psychologist treats a neurosis; an ophthalmologist treats a cataract.

266. e. A binding surrounds a book; a frame surrounds a picture.

267. b. One explores to discover; one researches to learn.

268. c. Upon harvesting, cotton is gathered into bales; grain is gathered into shocks.

269. a. Division and section are synonyms; layer and tier are synonyms.

270. a. Pastoral describes rural areas; metropolitan describes urban areas.

271. d. A waitress works in a restaurant; a teacher works in a school.

272. c. A finch is a type of bird; a Dalmatian is a type of dog.

273. e. To drizzle is to rain slowly; to jog is to run slowly.

274. c. A skein is a quantity of yarn; a ream is a quantity of paper.

275. b. To tailor a suit is to alter it; to edit a manuscript is to alter it.

▶ Set 17 (Page 41)

276. d. A conductor leads an orchestra; a skipper leads a crew.

277. a. Jaundice is an indication of a liver problem; rash is an indication of a skin problem.

278. b. A cobbler makes and repairs shoes; a contractor builds and repairs buildings.

279. e. To be phobic is to be extremely fearful; to be asinine is to be extremely silly.

280. c. Obsession is a greater degree of interest; fantasy is a greater degree of dream.

281. d. Devotion is characteristic of a monk; wanderlust is characteristic of a rover.

282. e. Slapstick results in laughter; horror results in fear.

283. b. Verve and enthusiasm are synonyms; devotion and reverence are synonyms.

284. c. A cacophony is an unpleasant sound; a stench is an unpleasant smell.

285. a. A conviction results in incarceration; a reduction results in diminution.

286. a. The deltoid is a muscle; the radius is a bone.

287. d. Umbrage and offense are synonyms; elation and jubilance are synonyms.

288. b. Being erudite is a trait of a professor; being imaginative is a trait of an inventor.

289. d. Dependable and capricious are antonyms; capable and inept are antonyms.

290. a. A palm (tree) has fronds; a porcupine has quills.

291. e. A metaphor is a symbol; an analogy is a comparison.

292. d. A dirge is a song used at a funeral; a jingle is a song used in a commercial.

293. e. Feral and tame are antonyms; ephemeral and immortal are antonyms.

294. a. A spy acts in a clandestine manner; an accountant acts in a meticulous manner.

295. c. Hegemony means dominance; autonomy means independence.

296. e. An aerie is where an eagle lives; a house is where a person lives.

▶ **Set 18** (Page 42)

297. a. *Grana* means big; *melke* means tree; *pini* means little; *hoon* means house. Therefore, *granahoon* means big house.

298. b. *Leli* means yellow; *broon* means hat; *pleka* means flower; *froti* means garden; *mix* means salad. Therefore, *lelipleka* means yellow flower.

299. d. From *wilkospadi,* you can determine that *wilko* means bicicyle and *spadi* means race. Therefore, the first part of the word that means racecar should begin with *spadi.* That limits your choices to **b** and **d.** Choice **b,** *spadiwilko,* is incorrect because we have already determined that *wilko* means bicycle. Therefore, the answer must be choice **d,** *spadivolo.*

300. a. *Dafta* means advise; *foni* is the same as the suffix –*ment*; *imo* is the same as the prefix *mis*–; *lokti* means conduct. Since the only word in the answer choices that hasn't been defined is *krata,* it is reasonable to assume that *krata* means state. Therefore, *kratafoni* is the only choice that could mean statement.

301. c. In this language, the adjective follows the noun. From *dionot* and *blyonot,* you can determine that *onot* means oak. From *blyonot* and *blycrin,* you can determine that *bly* means leaf. Therefore, *crin* means maple. Because the adjective maple comes after the noun, *patricrin* is the only possible choice.

302. c. In this language, the noun appears first and the adjectives follow. Since *agnos* means spider and should appear first, choices **a** and **d** can be ruled out. Choice **b** can be ruled out because *delano* means snake.

303. a. *Myn* means saddle; *cabel* means horse; *cono* means trail; and *wir* means ride. Therefore, *cabelwir* is the correct answer.

304. c. In this language, the adjective follows the noun. From *godabim* and *romzbim,* you can determine that *bim* means kidney. From *romzbim* and *romzbako,* you can determine that *romz* means beans. Therefore, *bako* means wax. Because the adjective wax must come after the noun, *wasibako* is the only choice.

305. b. *Tam* means sky; *ceno* means blue; *rax* means cheese; *apl* means star; and *mitl* means bright. So, *mitltam* means bright sky.

306. d. *Gorbl* means fan; *flur* means belt; *pixn* means ceiling; *arth* means tile; and *tusl* means roof. Therefore, *pixnarth* is the correct choice.

307. d. *Hapl* means cloud; *lesh* means burst; *srench* means pin; *och* means ball; and *resbo* means nine. *Leshsrench* (choice **a**) doesn't contain any of the words needed for cloud nine. We know that *och* means ball, so that rules out choices **b** and **c.** When you combine *hapl* (cloud) with *resbo* (nine), you get the correct answer.

308. d. *Migen* means cup; *lasan* means board; *poen* means walk; *cuop* means pull; and *dansa* means man. The only possible choices, then, are choices **a** and **d.** Choice **a** can be ruled out because *migen* means cup.

▶ Set 19 (Page 46)

309. c. *Morpir* means bird; *quat* means house; *beel* means blue; *clak* means bell. Choice **c**, which begins with *quat*, is the only possible option.

310. b. According to this language, *slar* means jump. The suffix *–ing* is represented by *–y*. Since choice **b** is the only one that ends in the letter *y*, this is the only possible option.

311. b. *Brift* means the root word *mili–*; the suffix *amint* means the same as the English suffix *–tant*; the root word *ufton–* means occupy; *el* means the suffix *–ied* of occupied; and *alene* means the suffix *–tion*. (Because *ufton* means occupy, choices **a**, **c**, and **d** can be easily ruled out.)

312. a. *Krekin* means work; *blaf* means force; *drita* means ground; and *alti* means place. *Drita* means ground, so that rules out choices **b** and **d**. Choice **c** isn't correct because *blaf* means force. That leaves choice **a** as the only possible answer.

313. d. *Pleka* means fruit; *paki* means cake; *shillen* means walk; *treft* means butter; and *alan* means cup. Therefore, *alanpaki* means cupcake.

314. b. *Pesl* means basketball; *ligen* means court; *strisi* means room; *olta* means placement; and *ganti* means test. Because *strisi* means room, it must be present in the answer, so that rules out choice **c**. Choices **a** and **d** are incorrect because *pesl* means basketball and *olta* means placement. That leaves choice **b** as the only possible answer.

315. a. *Jalka* means happy; *mofti* means birthday; *hoze* means party; *mento* means good; and *gunn* means the suffix *–ness*. We know the answer must include the suffix *–ness*. The only choice that uses that suffix is choice **a**.

316. d. *Mallon* means blue; *piml* means light; *tifl* means berry; and *arpan* means "rasp" in raspberry. The word *piml*, which means light, is required for the word lighthouse. That rules out choices **a** and **c**. *Arpan* in choice b means "rasp," so that rules out choice **b**. That leaves choice **d** the only possible answer.

317. a. *Gemo* means fair; *linea* means warning; *geri* means report; *mitu* means card; and *gila* means weather. Thus, *gemogila* is the correct choice.

318. d. *Apta* means first; *ose* means base; *epta* means second; *larta* means ball; and *buk* means park. Thus, *oselarta* means baseball.

319. c. In this language, the root word *taga*, which means care, follows the affix (*relf*, *o–*, or *fer–*). Therefore, in the word *aftercare*, the root word and the affix would be reversed in the artificial language. The only choice, then, is *tagazen*, because *tagafer* would mean less care.

320. a. *Malga* means peach; *uper* means cobbler; *port* means juice; *mogga* means apple; and *grop* means jelly. Therefore, *moggaport* means apple juice.

▶ **Set 20** (Page 48)

321.b. Valerie signed a legally binding document that requires her to pay a monthly rent for her apartment and she has failed to do this for the last three months. Therefore, she has violated her apartment lease.

322. a. Jake damaged Leslie's camera while it was in his possession and he has agreed to compensate Leslie for the cost of the repair.

323.d. This is the only situation in which someone makes an assumption that is not based on conclusive evidence. Choices **a** and **c** reflect situations in which assumptions are made based on evidence. In choice **b**, Mary is not assuming anything to be true. She is simply wishing that she'd made a different decision.

324.d. Choices **a**, **b**, and **c** do not describe situations in which a product is guaranteed. Only choice **d** reflects a situation in which a seller attests to the quality of a product by giving the buyer a promise or assurance about its quality.

325. c. Malcolm is the only person returning to a social system that he has been away from for an extended period of time.

326.b. The realtor is using a clear exaggeration when she states that a house which is eleven blocks away from the ocean is prime waterfront property.

327. c. Although the ski instructors at Top of the Peak Ski School do work seasonally, choice **a** does not describe anyone *applying* for seasonal employment. In choice **b**, the statement that Matthew likes to work outdoors tells us nothing about seasonal employment or someone applying for it. And although choice **d** describes a business with seasonal hours, it does not describe a person applying for seasonal work. Choice **c**, on the other hand, very specifically depicts a person, Lucinda, who is applying for a job as a summer waitress at a beach resort, which is dependent upon a particular season of the year.

328.b. After getting some good news, Jeremy and a few friends casually get together for a drink after work, thereby having an informal gathering. Choices **a** and **c** describe more formal types of gatherings. Choice **d** describes a chance or coincidental kind of meeting.

329. a. The fact that Jared is in scoring position due to his blooper indicates that he has hit the ball and is now a base runner; therefore, he has legally completed his time at bat. Choices **b** and **c** both describe situations in which a strike is called, but they do not state that the batter has been put out or that he is now a base runner. Choice **d** describes a situation in which the batter, Mario, is still at the plate waiting for the next pitch.

330. c. Although choices **a** and **c** both describe suspensions, only choice **c** describes a suspension that is the result of one of the two scenarios given in the definition of a five-day suspension (physical assault or destructing or defacing school property). Therefore, we can assume that Franny's suspension, which is the result of spray painting school property, will be a five-day suspension. Since the definition doesn't provide any information about suspensions for cheating, we can assume that Lillian's suspension does not fall into the five-day suspension category.

331.d. This is the only choice that indicates that an additional period of play is taking place to determine the winner of a game that ended in a tie.

332.b. Simone's mother has taken legal steps to allow another person to act on her behalf. Therefore, this is the only choice that indicates that a power of attorney has been established.

333.d. Jeffrey's recent behavior is clearly inconsistent and irregular.

334. a. Although choice **d** also mentions a writer who has died, it does not state that one of the writer's books was published after her death, only that she received an award. Choice **a** states that Richard wasn't around to see the early reviews of his novel, therefore implying that Richard died before the book was published. The other two options depict living writers.

► **Set 21** (Page 52)

335. b. Seeing four girls surrounding another girl, while in possession of her backpack, is the most suspicious of the incidents described.

336. b. The situation described indicates that Dr. Miller's practice presents some specific challenges, namely that it is a busy environment with a child clientele. There is also some indication that even highly recommended, experienced hygienists might not be cut out for Dr. Miller's office. There is nothing to suggest that Marilyn (choice **a**) or James (choice **c**) would be a good fit for Dr. Miller's practice. Kathy (choice **d**) has experience and she is also interested in working with children. However, the fact that she hopes to become a preschool teacher in the not-too-distant future indicates that she might not be the kind of committed, long-term employee that Dr. Miller needs. Lindy (choice **b**), with her hands-on experience working with children as well as a degree from a prestigious dental hygiene program, is the most attractive candidate for the position based on the situation described.

337. c. The Treehouse Collection is the only package that can thrive in shady locations. Choice **a** requires a Northeastern climate. Choices **b** and **d** require bright sunlight.

338. d. Since Eileen's husband does not enjoy fancy restaurants, choices **a** and **c** can be ruled out. Choice **b**, although casual, doesn't sound as though it would be the kind of special and memorable evening that Eileen is looking for. Choice **d**, which is owned by a former baseball star and is described as "charming" and "reminiscent of a baseball clubhouse," sounds perfect for Eileen's husband, who is described as a baseball fan and a man with simple tastes.

339. b. This option is both near the center of town and in a location (near a school and an ice cream store) where children and their parents are sure to be around. This is the only option that meets both of Mark's requirements.

340. c. This is the only option that would encourage people to think of the bakery as a shop they would visit regularly and not just on special occasions.

341. a. The four women seem to agree that the plate starts out with the letter J. Three of them agree that the plate ends with 12L. Three of them think that the second letter is X, and a different three think that the third letter is K. The plate description that has all of these common elements is **a**.

342. a. All of the men agree that the first three numbers are 995. Three of them agree that the fourth number is 9. Three agree that the fifth number is 2. Three agree that the sixth number is 6; three others agree that the seventh number is also 6. Choice **a** is the best choice because it is made up of the numbers that most of the men agree they saw.

343. d. Step 4 clearly states that the human resources representative should issue the new employee a temporary identification card.

344. c. Step 2 of the guidelines states that the realtor should get background information about the client's current living circumstances. Ms. Russo failed to do this.

345. b. Actresses #2 and #3 possess most of the required traits. They both have red hair and brown eyes, are average-sized, and are in their forties. Actress #1 is very tall and is only in her mid-twenties. She also has an olive complexion. Actress #4 is of very slight build and is in her early thirties. She also has blue eyes.

346. c. The solicitor described as #2 has a shaved head and is much taller and heavier than the solicitors described as #1 and #3. Therefore, choices **a** and **d**, which include #2, can be ruled out. Solicitors #1, #3, and #4 have such similar descriptions that the correct answer is clearly choice **c**.

► **Set 22** (Page 57)

347. c. Since Erin's parents think a dog would not be happy in an apartment, we can reasonably conclude that the family lives in an apartment. We do not know if Erin's parents dislike dogs (choice **a**) or if Erin dislikes birds (choice **b**). There is no support for choice **d**.

348. d. It is reasonable to conclude that Mike likes singing and dancing because he looks forward to doing these things at music camp. There is no information that supports any of the other three choices.

349. c. Given the information presented, the only statement that could be considered true is that the fruit should not be eaten because it is poisonous. There is no support that taxol is poisonous or that taxol has cured anyone (choices **a** and **b**). There is no support for choice **d**.

350. a. Because Mr. Sanchez spends many hours during the weekend working in his vegetable garden, it is reasonable to suggest that he enjoys this work. There is no information to suggest that he does not like classical music. Although Mrs. Sanchez likes to cook, there is nothing that indicates she cooks vegetables (choice **c**). Mrs. Sanchez likes to read, but there is no information regarding the types of books she reads (choice **d**).

351. b. The passage tells us that Tim's commute didn't bother him because he was always able to sit down and comfortably read or do paperwork. Therefore, it is reasonable to assume that Tim's commute has become less comfortable since the schedule change, because it is very crowded and he can no longer find a seat. There is no information given that supports choices **a**, **c**, and **d**.

352. d. The first sentence makes this statement true. There is no support for choice **a**. The passage tells us that the spa vacation is more expensive than the island beach resort vacation, but that doesn't necessarily mean that the spa is overpriced; therefore, choice **b** cannot be supported. And even though the paragraph says that the couple was relieved to find a room on short notice, there is no information to support choice **c**, which says that it is usually necessary to book at the spa at least six months in advance.

353. b. Since the seahorse populations have declined as a result of fishing, their populations will increase if seahorse fishing is banned. There is no support for any of the other choices.

354. a. The fact that Vincent and Thomas live on the same street indicates that they live in the same neighborhood. There is no support for any of the other choices.

355. d. If Georgia is older than Marsha and Bart is older than Georgia, then Marsha has to be the youngest of the three. Choice **b** is clearly wrong because Bart is the oldest. There is no information in the paragraph to support either choice **a** or choice **c**.

356. c. If there were seven shows left and five were sitcoms, this means that only two of the shows could possibly be dramas. Choices **a** and **b** may be true, but there is no evidence to indicate this as fact. The fact that all of the sitcoms remained does not necessarily mean that viewers prefer sitcoms (choice **d**).

357. c. Since the paragraph states that Marlee is the younger cousin, Sara must be older than Marlee. There is no information to support the other choices.

▶ **Set 23** (Page 60)

358. b. Because the first two statements are true, Eric is the youngest of the three, so the third statement must be false.

359. c. Because the first two sentences are true, both Josh and Darren saw more movies than Stephen. However, it is uncertain as to whether Darren saw more movies than Josh.

360. c. The first two statements give information about Zoe's tulips and pansies. Information about any other kinds of flowers cannot be determined.

361. a. Because the first two statements are true, raspberries are the most expensive of the three.

362. a. If no wall-to-wall carpeting is pink and all the offices have wall-to-wall carpeting, none of the offices has pink wall-to-wall carpeting.

363. b. From the first two statements, we know that of the three classes, Class A has the highest enrollment, so the third statement must be false.

364. a. According to the first two statements, Fido weighs the most and Boomer weighs the least.

365. c. Although all of the trees in the park are flowering trees, it cannot be determined by the information given whether all dogwoods are flowering trees.

366. a. Since the Gaslight Commons costs more than the Riverdale Manor and the Livingston Gate costs more than the Gaslight Commons, it is true that the Livingston Gate costs the most.

367. a. From the first two statements, you know that the Kingston Mall has the most stores, so the Kingston Mall would have more stores than the Four Corners Mall.

368. b. We know from the first two statements that Lily runs fastest. Therefore, the third statement must be false.

▶ Set 24 (Page 62)

369. a. From the first statement, we know that bran cereal has more fiber than both oat cereal and corn cereal. From the second statement, we know that rice cereal has less fiber than both corn and wheat cereals. Therefore, rice cereal has the least amount of fiber.

370. c. We only know that Jasmine weighs more than Jason. There is no way to tell whether Jasmine also weighs more than Jenna.

371. c. We know from the first two statements that Tuesday had the highest temperature, but we cannot know whether Monday's temperature was higher than Tuesday's.

372. b. Spot is bigger than King, and Ralph is bigger than Spot. Therefore, King must be smaller than Ralph.

373. a. There are fewer oranges than either apples or lemons, so the statement is true.

374. b. Because the first two statements are true, Rebecca's house is also northeast of the Shop and Save Grocery, which means that the third statement is false.

375. a. Joe is younger than Kathy and older than Mark, so Mark must be younger than Kathy.

376. c. We know only that long-tailed Gangles have spots. We cannot know for certain if long-tailed Gangles also have short hair.

377. c. The first two statements indicate that Battery Y lasts the least amount of time, but it cannot be determined if Battery Z lasts longer than Battery X.

378. b. Given the information in the first two statements, Bryant is sitting in front of both Jerome and Martina, so the third statement must be false.

379. b. Because the first two statements are true, Penfield is west of Centerville and southwest of Middletown. Therefore, the third statement is false.

► **Set 25** (Page 64)

380. c. Both the car and the train are quicker than the bus, but there is no way to make a comparison between the train and the car.

381. a. We know that there are Signots with buttons, or Lamels, and that there are yellow Signots, which have no buttons. Therefore, Lamels do not have buttons and cannot be yellow.

382. a. The market is one block west of the hotel. The drugstore is two blocks west of the hotel, so the drugstore is west of the market.

383. c. There is not enough information to verify the third statement.

384. b. Rulers are the most expensive item.

385. b. The first two statements indicate there are more yellow jelly beans than red and green.

386. c. Cloudy days are the most windy, but there is not enough information to compare the wind on the foggy days with the wind on the sunny days.

387. a. Of the three, the drugstore has the best selection of postcards.

388. b. This is the order of the cars from left to right: minivan, pickup, sedan, sport utility vehicle.

389. a. To the extent that a toothpick is useful, it has value.

▶ **Set 26** (Page 66)

390. a. Since one-half of the four children are girls, two must be boys. It is not clear which children have blue or brown eyes.

391. d. All baseball caps have brims, since baseball caps are hats (Fact 3) and all hats have brims (Fact 1). This rules out statement III—but it doesn't follow that all caps, a category that may include caps that are not baseball caps, have brims (statement I). Statement II cannot be confirmed, either, since it is possible, given the information, that all baseball caps are black.

392. b. The first statement cannot be true because only female birds lay eggs. Statement II is true because hens are chickens and chickens are birds. Statement III is also true because if only some chickens are hens, then some must not be hens.

393. d. None of the three statements is supported by the known facts.

394. c. Statements I and II are not supported by the facts. Statement III is true because if all storybooks have pictures and only some have words, then some storybooks have both words and pictures.

395. d. There is not enough information to support any of the statements. Robert is known to have a minvan, but it is not known which of his vehicles is red. Robert may have a pickup or sport utility vehicle, so the second statement cannot be supported. There is no way to know if Robert's favorite color is red (statement III).

396. a. Since Maui is an island and islands are surrounded by water, Maui must be surrounded by water. There is not enough information to support statements II and III.

397. c. If all drink mixes are beverages and some beverages are red, then some drink mixes are red (statement I). Since all beverages are drinkable and all drink mixes are beverages, then all red drink mixes must be drinkable (statement III). Statement II can be ruled out.

398. d. There is no information in the facts to support statements I or II. Statement III is clearly wrong because, according to Fact 1, no frames cost less than $35.

399. b. Since some pens don't write, some writing utensils don't write (statement I). Since there are blue pens and since pens are writing utensils, some writing utensils are blue (statement II). There is not enough information to support statement III.

400. c. If Mary always tells the truth, then both Ann and Mary have cats (statements I and II), and Ann is lying (statement III).

401. b. Statement II is the only true statement. Since all dogs like to run, then the ones who like to swim also like to run. There is no support for statement I or statement III.

▶ **Set 27** (Page 69)

402. d. After all the switches were made, Max is directly behind the dog, James is alongside the dog on the left, Ruby is alongside the dog on the right, and Rachel is behind Max.

403. b. Nurse Kemp has worked more shifts in a row than Nurse Calvin; therefore, Kemp has worked more than eight shifts. The number of Kemp's shifts plus the number of Rogers's shifts (five) cannot equal fifteen or more, the number of Miller's shifts. Therefore, Kemp has worked nine shifts in a row $(5 + 9 = 14)$.

404. c. If Randy is two months older than Greg, then Ned is three months older than Greg and one month older than Randy. Kent is younger than both Randy and Ned. Ned is the oldest.

405. c. After all the switches were made, Shawn is in front of the house. Ross is in the alley behind the house, Michael is on the north side, and Jed is on the south.

406. d. After all the switches were made, Mr. Kirk worked on Tuesday. Mr. Carter worked on Monday, Ms. Johnson on Wednesday, and Ms. Falk on Thursday.

407. a. Mr. Temple has the most seniority, but he does not want the job. Next in line is Mr. Rhodes, who has more seniority than Ms. West or Ms. Brody.

408. b. Tall, thin, and middle-aged are the elements of the description repeated most often and are therefore the most likely to be accurate.

409. b. Beth won the biggest prize, described as a higher medal than Jamie's, which we've been told was a silver medal. Roberta and Michele both won bronze medals, which are lower ranking medals than silver. Beth is also described as having competed more times than Roberta—who has competed seven times. Jamie is described as having competed fewer times than Roberta, and Michele has competed three times. Therefore, Beth has competed more times than the others and has won the biggest prize to date.

410. c. After all the switching was done, Jenkins was directly behind the receiver. Calvin and Burton had fallen. Zeller remained in the rear.

411. d. Alexis is farther away than Frances, who is five miles away, and closer than Samantha, who is seven miles away.

412. a. Baxter should be assigned to study with Carter. Baxter cannot be assigned with Adam, because they have already been together for seven class periods. If Baxter is assigned to work with Dennis, that would leave Adam with Carter, but Carter does not want to work with Adam.

413. a. If George is sitting at Henry's left, George's seat is 252. The next seat to the left, then, is 251.

► **Set 28** (Page 72)

414. d. The total of the three programs (2 million + 0.5 million + 3 million) is 5.5 million. That leaves 1.5 million (7 million − 5.5 million), and the only single program needing that amount is the senate office building remodeling.

415. b. The only two programs that total 1.5 million dollars are the harbor improvements and school music program.

416. a. The total cost of the school music program and national radio is $1 million, the amount left after the international airport and agricultural subsidies are funded.

417. c. J will only work in episodes in which M is working and there are no restrictions on O's schedule. However, N will not work with K, so M must appear and O may appear.

418. d. K will not work with N, so choices **c** and **e** are incorrect. M can only work every other week, so choice **a** is incorrect. Since M is not working, J will not work, so choice **b** is incorrect.

419. b. Only choice **b** contains no more than two R-rated movies (*Shout* and *Mist*), at least one G and one PG (*Fly, Abra Cadabra,* and *Jealousy*), and only one foreign film (*Mist*).

420. c. The first showing of *Trek* will be over at 10:00. Then, the employees will need 20 minutes to clean the theater, which is 10:20. Since the movies always start on the quarter hour, the second showing of *Trek* will be 10:30.

421. e. Since *Shout* is doing the most business and *Trek* the second most, they should remain in the two largest theaters. Also, the theater never shows a foreign film in the largest theater. Theaters 3 and 4 must show the movies that are rated G and PG, so the movies that are there must stay there. The most logical choice is to put *Mist* in theater 5 and *Fly* in theater 6.

422. a. "Honey" and "Sittin' on the Dock of the Bay" are either 3 and 4 or 4 and 3. The Rascals appear on the list right after Otis Redding, who cannot be #3 (or he would be followed by Bobby Goldsboro), so "Honey" is #3 and "Sittin' on the Dock of the Bay" is #4; therefore, choices **c** and **e** are incorrect. The Rascals are #5 (because they are right after Otis Redding), and Cream appears right after them, so choice **d** is incorrect. Since Cream has song #6, it cannot be "Hey Jude," so choice **b** is incorrect.

423. d. In the previous question, it was determined that #3 is "Honey," #4 is "Sittin' on the Dock of the Bay," #5 is "People Got to Be Free," and #6 is "Sunshine of Your Love." Since the #1 song is not "Love Is Blue," #1 is "Hey Jude," and #2 is "Love Is Blue."

▶ **Set 29** (Page 76)

Here's a quick illustration of how to work "logic game" puzzles, using the situation in questions 424 and 425 as an example.

First, read the paragraph. Then, construct a diagram or table like the one below. Write down the letters that represent the names of the people at the party. Next, add any other information that is given. You know that Quentin is an accountant and Sarah is a florist; you know which objects represent their type of work. You also know that Thomas is dressed as a camera, so he must be the photographer.

Q	accountant	pencil
R		
S	florist	flower
T	photographer	camera
U		

Since none of the men is a doctor, Rachel must be the doctor. That leaves Ulysses, who must be the chef. Once you've filled in your diagram and made the deductions, answering the questions is the easy part.

Q	accountant	pencil
R	*doctor*	*thermometer*
S	florist	flower
T	photographer	camera
U	*chef*	*spoon*

424. b. See the table above. The thermometer costume logically would be worn by the doctor. According to the information, none of the men is a doctor. Also, Sarah is a florist, so Rachel must be the doctor wearing the thermometer costume.

425. e. Ulysses cannot be a doctor, because that is Rachel. Quentin is an accountant, Thomas must be a photographer, and Sarah is a florist. That leaves chef for Ulysses. We also know the chef must be a man, because neither of the women is dressed as a spoon.

426. d. The person who ordered the vegetable burger cannot be sitting in chairs 1 or 6, because she is sitting between two people. She also cannot be sitting in chairs 3 or 4, because those customers did not order sandwiches. Since she is not sitting in chair 2, she must be in chair 5.

427. c. The customer who ordered soup must be in chair 3 or 4, where the non-sandwich orders go. The other non-sandwich order is fried eggs, and that person is sitting next to the customer in chair 5 (who ordered the vegetable burger), so the fried eggs go to chair 4 and the soup to chair 3.

428. b. The orders that go to chairs 3, 4, 5, and 6 are already determined, so the ham sandwich must go to chair 1 or 2. The customer who ordered the hamburger is not sitting next to the person who ordered the soup in chair 3, so the hamburger must go to chair 1 and the ham sandwich to chair 2.

429. a. The person who ordered potato salad cannot be in chair 1 or 6, since he is sitting between two people. The person who ordered fried eggs ordered hash browns and is sitting in chair 4. The person who ordered potato salad is on one side of chair 4, either 3 or 5. He cannot be in chair 5 and still be next to both the hash browns and the cole slaw, so he must be in chair 3, which is where the soup was ordered.

430. c. If the potato salad is with the soup and the hash browns are with the fried eggs, then the cole slaw must be with the ham sandwich, in chairs 2, 3, and 4. The lettuce salad is with the vegetable burger in chair 5. The onion rings belong to the cheeseburger in chair 6, leaving the french fries for the hamburger in chair 1.

431. a. The vice president's car cannot be red, because that is the CEO's car, which is in the first space. Nor can it be purple, because that is the treasurer's car, which is in the last space, or yellow, because that is the secretary's. The president's car must be blue, because it is parked between a red car (in the first space) and a green car, which must be the vice president's.

432. c. The CEO drives a red car and parks in the first space. Enid drives a green car; Bert's car is not in the first space; David's is not in the first space, but the last. Alice's car is parked next to David's, so Cheryl is the CEO.

433. e. Cheryl cannot be the secretary, since she's the CEO, nor can Enid, because she drives a green car, and the secretary drives a yellow car. David's, the purple car, is in the last space. Alice is the secretary, because her car is parked next to David's, which is where the secretary's car is parked.

▶ **Set 30** (Page 79)

434. d. The Whippets cannot be in Jersey, Hudson, or Fulton, since they have beaten those teams. The Antelopes are in Groton, so the Whippets are in Ivy.

435. e. The Panthers cannot be in Ivy or Groton, because the Whippets and Antelopes are there. Fulton has beaten the Panthers, so they cannot be in Fulton. Fulton has also beaten the Kangaroos, so the only town left for the Kangaroos is Jersey. That leaves Hudson for the Panthers.

436. b. Every team and town is matched up, except Fulton and the Gazelles, so the Gazelles must be in Fulton.

437. a. Kevin is allergic to daisies and iris; he's not getting gladioli because it's not his housewarming. The roses are going to Jenny, leaving the carnations for Kevin.

438. d. Jenny is getting roses and Kevin is getting carnations. Neither Liz nor Inez would be getting a housewarming present. Michael is getting gladioli.

439. e. The only flowers unassigned are iris and daisies. Liz is allergic to daisies, so she is getting the iris.

440. e. The city that got the least rain is in the desert. New Town is in the mountains. Last Stand got more rain than Olliopolis, so it cannot be the city with the least rain; also, Mile City cannot be the city with the least rain. Olliopolis got 44 inches of rain. Therefore, Polberg is in the desert and got 12 inches of rain.

441. a. Olliopolis got 44 inches of rain. Last Stand got more rain than that, so it got 65 inches, which is the most.

442. b. Olliopolis got 44 inches of rain, Last Stand got 65, and Polberg got 12. New Town is in the mountains, and the city in the mountains got 32 inches of rain. Therefore, Mile City got 27.

443. c. Olliopolis got 44 inches of rain, so it is not in the desert or the forest. The city in the mountains got 32 inches of rain; the coast 27. Therefore, Olliopolis is in a valley.

► Set 31 (Page 81)

444. d. The moderator sits in seat #3. It cannot, then, be Gary or Jarrod or Lane, who sit next to the moderator. Heloise is not the moderator; therefore, the moderator is Kate.

445. a. Jarrod cannot sit in seat #3 because he is not the moderator. Nor can he sit in seat #2 or #4, because he does not sit next to the moderator. Heloise cannot sit on an end, nor in seat #3 or #4, so she is in seat #2, between the moderator (Kate) and Jarrod, who must be in seat #1.

446. e. Jarrod sits in seat #1 and is not the moderator; nor is he the pilot or the attorney. The attorney sits in seat #4 and cannot sit next to the explorer. Therefore, the pilot, Lane, is in seat #5, and the explorer must be in seat #1, Jarrod's seat.

447. b. Jarrod is the explorer, Lane is the pilot, Kate is the moderator, and Gary is the attorney. Heloise must be the writer.

448. d. Zinnia plants tomatoes each year, so choice **e** is incorrect. Each year, she plants either carrots or cabbage, but not both. She will plant cabbage in the second year, so she will plant carrots in the first. She never plants carrots and peppers together, so the first year is tomatoes, carrots, beans and the second is tomatoes, cabbage, peppers.

449. c. Dusting must be done on Tuesday, Wednesday, or Thursday. However, the mopping is done on Thursday, and Terry does his task on Wednesday. Therefore, Sally does the dusting on Tuesday.

450. d. Terry does not dust, mop, do laundry, or vacuum. Therefore, Terry does the sweeping on Wednesday.

451. b. Dusting is on Tuesday, sweeping is on Wednesday, mopping is on Thursday, and laundry is on Friday. Therefore, the vacuuming is done on Monday.

452. e. Vernon does not vacuum, dust, or sweep. Randy does the vacuuming, Sally does the dusting, Terry does the sweeping—leaving laundry and mopping for Uma and Vernon. Uma does not do laundry; therefore, she must mop, and Vernon does the laundry.

453. d. Uma does the mopping, which is done on Thursday.

▶ **Set 32** (Page 83)

454. d. By stating that fitness walking does not require a commute to a health club, the author stresses the convenience of this form of exercise. The paragraph also states that fitness walking will result in a good workout. Choice **a** is incorrect because no comparison to weight lifting is made. Choice **b** may seem like a logical answer, but the paragraph only refers to people who are fitness walkers, so for others, a health club might be a good investment. Choice **c** is not in the passage. Although choice **e** seems logical, the paragraph does not indicate that the wrong shoes will produce major injuries.

455. e. This answer is implied by the statement that redistribution is needed so that people in emerging nations can have proper medical care. Choices **a**, **b**, and **c** are not mentioned in the passage. Choice **d** is also incorrect—the passage indicates that the distribution of medicine, not its production, is inadequate.

456. b. This answer is clearly stated in the first sentence of the paragraph. There is no support in the passage for choices **a**, **d**, or **e**. As for choice **c**, although mediation is mentioned, the statement does not indicate that victims should be the mediators.

457. c. This choice is supported as the best answer because the paragraph indicates that low-fat ice cream was once an unpopular item, but now, because consumers are more health conscious and because there is a wider array of tasty low-fat foods, low-fat ice cream is a profitable item for ice cream store owners. There is no indication that choices **a**, **b**, **d**, or **e** are true based on the information given.

458. a. The paragraph clearly states that there are two differing opinions with regard to the use of calculators in the classroom. Although some people may believe that choice **b** is true, the paragraph does not indicate this. Choice **c** has no relation to the paragraph. Choice **d** makes logical sense, but the paragraph says nothing about cost. Choice **e** is an opinion that is not given in the paragraph.

459. e. This is clearly the best answer because the paragraph directly states that warm weather affects consumers' inclination to spend. It furthers states that the sales of single-family homes was at an all-time high. There is no support for choice **a** or **c**. Choice **b** is wrong because even though there were high sales for a particular February, this does not mean that sales are not higher in other months. Choice **d** presents a misleading figure of 4 million. The paragraph states that the record of 4.75 million was at an annual, not a monthly, rate.

460. b. The last sentence in the paragraph clearly gives support for the idea that the interest in Shakespeare is due to the development of his characters. Choice **a** is incorrect because the writer never makes this type of comparison. Choice **c** is wrong because even though scholars are mentioned in the paragraph, there is no indication that the scholars are compiling the anthology. Choice **d** is wrong because there is no support to show that most New Yorkers are interested in this work. There is no support for choice **e** either.

461. c. A change in employee social values over the past ten years is implied in the whole paragraph, but particularly in the first sentence. Choice **a** is incorrect because the loyalty of the managers to their corporations is never discussed. There is no support for choice **b**. In choice **d**, perhaps career advancement is less important than it once was, but the paragraph does not indicate that advancement is unimportant to managers. Choice **e** is an opinion that is not supported.

462. b. The support for choice **b** is given in the second sentence of the paragraph. Generation Xers like to work independently, which means they are self-directed. No support is given for either choice **a** or choice **c**. Choice **d** is not related to the paragraph. Although the paragraph mentions that Generation Xers like to be challenged, it does not say they like to challenge their bosses' attitudes; therefore, choice **e** can be ruled out.

463. e. The support for choice **e** is in the third sentence ". . . we should make school uniforms mandatory." There is no evidence provided to support choices **a**, **b**, and **d**. And although we know that teachers and administrators are spending some of their time enforcing dress code, the paragraph does not quantify how much of their time is spent that way, so there is no support for choice **c**.

► Set 33 (Page 86)

464. d. This answer is implied by the whole paragraph. The author stresses the need to read critically by performing thoughtful and careful operations on the text. Choice **a** is incorrect because the author never says that reading is dull. Choices **b**, **c**, and **e** are not supported by the paragraph.

465. a. The support for this choice is in the second sentence, which states that in some countries, toxic insecticides are still legal. Choice **b** is incorrect because even though polar regions are mentioned in the paragraph, there is no support for the idea that warmer regions are not just as affected. There is no support for choice **c**. Choice **d** can be ruled out because there is nothing to indicate that DDT and toxaphene are the *most* toxic. Choice **e** is illogical.

466. a. The second and third sentence combine to give support to choice **a**. The statement stresses that there must be a judge's approval (i.e., legal authorization) before a search can be conducted. Choices **b** and **d** are wrong because it is not enough for the police to have direct evidence or a reasonable belief—a judge must authorize the search for it to be legal. Choices **c** and **e** are not mentioned in the passage.

467. e. The paragraph focuses on the idea that the jury system is different from what it was in colonial times. There is no support given for choices **a**, **b**, and **c**. Choice **d** is incorrect because, even though jurors in colonial times were expected to investigate and ask questions, this does not necessarily mean that they were more informed than today's jurors.

468. e. This answer is clearly stated in the last sentence of the paragraph. Choice **a** can be ruled out because there is no support to show that study-ing math is dangerous. Words are not mentioned in the passage, which rules out choice **b**. Choice **d** is a contradiction to the information in the passage. There is no support for choice **c**.

469. d. The last sentence states that new technologies are reported daily, and this implies that new technologies are being constantly developed. There is no support for choice **a**. With regard to choice **b**, stone tools were first used two and a half million years ago, but they were not necessarily in use all that time. Choice **c** is clearly wrong since the paragraph states when stone tools first came into use. Although some may agree that choice **e** is true, the author of the paragraph does not give support for this opinion.

470. a. The support for this choice is in the last sentence, which states that major public health campaigns that increase awareness and propose lifestyle changes are important in our fight against obesity. Choice **b** can be ruled out because although the paragraph states that obesity can lead to diabetes, it doesn't tell us that it is the leading cause of this disease. Choices **c** and **e** might sound reasonable and true, but they are not supported in the paragraph. And although we are told that obesity has been connected to asthma, this fact is not quantified in any way, so choice **d** is also not supported by the information given.

471. b. This answer is clearly supported in the second sentence. Nothing in the paragraph suggests that it is a crime not to give a Miranda warning, so choice **a** is incorrect. Choice **c** is also wrong because police may interrogate as long as a warning is given. There is no support given for either choice **d** or **e**.

ANSWERS

472. c. The last sentence gives direct support for this response. Although children might be better protected from the sun than adults, the paragraph does not specifically cite statistics about children, so we can't know for sure, ruling out choice **a**. There is no evidence provided in the paragraph to support choices **b** and **d**. Choice **e** is incorrect since the last sentence tells us that warnings about the sun's dangers are frequent.

473. b. The second sentence points out that people should examine what they want from a fitness routine before signing up for a new exercise class. There is no evidence to support choice **a**. Choice **c** might sound reasonable due to the fact that the paragraph tells us that yoga has become very popular, but this statement is not supported by the information provided in the paragraph. Choices **d** and **e** are also not supported since the paragraph doesn't tell us whether yoga is good for both body and mind or what people think about it.

► **Set 34** (Page 90)

474. d. The final sentence of the paragraph supports choice **d**. The other choices are not supported by the passage. Choice **c** may seem correct at first, but the paragraph states that the new initiatives are simple and inexpensive, not major. Choice **e** might seem to represent a truth, but vegetarian options are not discussed in this paragraph.

475. d. The author of this statement suggests that doctors are less independent. The author stresses that many doctors have lost authority. There is no support for the opinion that doctors resent the healthcare managers, however—which rules out choice **a**. The doctors' training is never mentioned (choice **b**). Doctors may care about their patients (choice **c**), but this information is not part of the paragraph. Choice **e** is not mentioned.

476. e. The second sentence states that threading a needle involves motor skill. The other choices are not in the paragraph.

477. a. The paragraph states that Mars once had a thick atmosphere, but that it was stripped away. The other choices, true or not, cannot be found in the passage.

478. a. The last sentence provides direct support for choice **a**. The author never suggests that any trees should be cut down or thinned out, which eliminates choices **b** and **c**. Choice **d** contradicts the author's opinion. The author suggests that old growth forests have less debris, which rules out choice **e**.

479. c. The fact that the Pyramid scheme is set up by a con artist suggests that the honest people who invest have been fooled. Choices **a** and **b** are contradicted in the passage. The paragraph says that the Pyramid scheme originated in the 1920s, but does not say it had its heyday then; thus, choice **d** is incorrect. Choice **e** is a fact, but it is not mentioned in the passage.

480. a. This is expressed in the first sentence. Choices **b**, **d**, and **e** are not supported by the passage. Choice **c** is incorrect because the paragraph states that some Reality TV stars manage to parlay their fifteen minutes of fame into celebrity.

481. c. The statement that it is difficult to create an accurate profile of a contemporary knitter comes immediately after a discussion about how different today's knitters are from one another and from knitters of the past. Choices **a** and **d** are not supported by the paragraph. Although the paragraph does discuss knitting done in group settings, it does not specifically say that more of today's knitting is done in groups; therefore, choice **b** is incorrect. Young people may be turning to knitting in record numbers, but again, that statement is not verified by the information provided in the paragraph, so choice **e** must be ruled out as well.

▶ **Set 35** (Page 93)

482. b. If it is more expensive to run a medical practice in a large city than a small town, it would make sense for doctors to charge more in large cities. Choices **a**, **c**, and **e** are incorrect because the information in these statements is extraneous to the author's argument. Choice **d** is wrong because it supports, rather than refutes, the author's argument.

483. e. The passage states that "doctors in large cities make more money than doctors in small towns or rural areas." The speaker then assumes that if doctors all charge the same, they will all earn the same, but if doctors in large cities see more patients, they will still earn more money.

484. a. The argument is based on the idea that the government spends a great deal of money translating documents into different languages. Choices **b** and **e** make the argument somewhat weaker. Choice **c** offers no support for the argument. Choice **d** may offer some support, but choice **a** makes the argument much stronger.

485. c. If most people learn English within a short period of time, making English the official language is unnecessary.

486. d. The speaker maintains that to burn a flag is an act of freedom of speech, which is among the things the flag represents.

487. a. If an action is not included under freedom of speech, the speaker's main argument is incorrect.

488. b. This is the best choice because it relates to a situation where a proposed law would actually violate the part of the Constitution it is intended to protect.

▶ **Set 36** (Page 95)

489. a. Because the speaker is arguing that multiple guests should be allowed when fewer members are present, the purpose of the rule is to make sure members are not crowded by the presence of guests. There is no support for choices **b**, **c**, or **d**. Choice **e** is attractive, but it is not the best choice because there is no way the club could control which members would be at the club at any one time.

490. c. Joint pain caused by physical activity and that caused by arthritis may not respond the same way to medication.

491. e. This would indicate that the conditions of the football players and the speaker's mother are similar.

492. c. The speaker uses analogies to compare crawling with learning arithmetic and reading and to compare walking with using a computer. The speaker is making the point that, in both cases, a child needs to learn one before learning the other.

493. e. This evidence would back up the speaker's contention that young students should learn the basics before learning computers. Choices **a** and **d**, which are both about cost, would have no effect on the argument. Choices **b** and **c** are too vague.

494. a. If computers enhance the learning of arithmetic and reading, the speaker's argument is not as strong.

495. b. The speaker refers to the safety of children because most people are concerned about that. The speaker does not make a comparison (choice **a**). Choice **c** can be ruled out because the speaker does not give a specific number. Choices **d** and **e** are incorrect because the speaker doesn't give an account of any specific child, nor does he or she use any method of attack.

496. e. Since the speaker is basing the argument on the safety of children, if there were only a few accidents and none involved children, the argument is weaker.

▶ **Set 37** (Page 97)

497.b. Lars provides information that supports Frances's more general statements. Both agree that schools should spend money on educating children, not on providing breakfast. Choices **a**, **d**, and **e** are incorrect because they all imply that Frances and Lars are arguing in opposition to each other. Choice **c** can be ruled out because Lars's position does not give any outcomes.

498.d. Both speakers rely on the fact that schools do not traditionally have the responsibility for providing students with breakfast.

499.d. The speakers support their arguments in different ways, but both are concerned with whether sixteen-year-olds should continue to be allowed to receive drivers' licenses.

500. c. Quinn discusses the fairness of changing the law and raising the age at which one can receive a driver's license. Emotion (choice **b**) may be involved, but the argument relies on the fairness issue.

501. e. Dakota discusses the actualities of increased traffic and the decline in the teaching of drivers' education. She doesn't use statistics (choice **a**). Her argument is not emotion-filled, which rules out choice **b**. She doesn't mention fairness (choice **c**) and doesn't tell stories about specific situations (choice **d**).

NOTES

NOTES

NOTES

NOTES